CASES
in Financial
Management

ROBERT STRETCHER
TIMOTHY B. MICHAEL

PEARSON

Prentice
Hall

Upper Saddle River

Acquisitions Editor: David Alexander
Editor-in-Chief: Jeff Shelstad
Assistant Editor: Francesca Calogero
Executive Marketing Manager: Sharon Koch
Managing Editor: John Roberts
Permissions Supervisor: Charles Morris
Manufacturing Buyer: Michelle Klein
Cover Design: Bruce Kenselaar
Printer/Binder: Phoenix Book Tech

10 9 8 7 6 5 4 3 2
ISBN 0-13-148343-9

CONTENTS

Section 4. Capital Budgeting Decisions 59

Section 5. Leverage and Risk 99

Section 6. Cost of Capital 107

Section 7. Working Capital Management 125

Preface

Experiential Learning and Case Studies

The meaning, application, and nature of case studies differ greatly across textbooks, authors, universities, and disciplines. In some environments, case studies are essentially reality, such as in medical training. In the finance classroom, it is difficult to bring reality to the place of learning. To some degree, though, case studies make this possible, while maintaining the absence of serious penalties for errors that are present "on the job." Typically, a business case provides a set of narrated facts that describe a real situation. You are required to observe, structure, and analyze the situation, synthesizing the relevant case information using tools or theories from their discipline. The objective is to engage you and your peers in a business situation, allowing you to practice theories, principles, and techniques that are emphasized in a class. This permits you to move from conceptual textbook material into an applied learning experience.

Cases are unlike "back of the book" problems. The real world often does not fit nicely into the academic finance models. Since financial management is an applied discipline, it is important to provide for experiential learning. Experiential learning can be accomplished with internships and co-ops. However, these do not usually provide for exposure to a wide variety of financial situations where you can practice the principles of your academic learning. The responsibility level of internships and co-ops is also normally on the low end, separating interns from financially responsible decisions the firm must make. Cases, though, can effectively present a variety of nuances for advanced students, or can focus on more narrow lessons for the beginner. A wide set of experiences can challenge you and can produce competencies that are retained beyond your academic world and utilized on the job.

Cases often do not have "correct" solutions. Even experts in the field realize that the success of a properly applied recommendation depends on factors that cannot be predicted with confidence. In financial management, decision techniques are most often based on expectations. Expectations, of course, may not pan out. For this reason, professors are typically more interested in what you can assess in your case analysis: your use of facts, diagnosis of the issue(s), proper application of theories and tools, ability to make decisions with incomplete information, and development of a sound argument consistent with the facts to support your recommendation.

The case study approach in training practitioners is widely recognized and has become increasingly applied to the training of attorneys, physicians, nurses, and other professionals. Even in business cases, the analogy is that of a medical diagnosis. A physician observes symptoms, runs tests, summarizes information on a chart, and determines treatments and medications that are proper for the situation. Similarly, the finance student can observe the case symptoms (facts) facing the patient (a business, manager, or individual). For example, a firm may be experiencing declining profits, loss of market share, and high employee turnover. The task of the student is to identify the underlying problem causing these troubling facts. It would be ridiculous for a physician to treat an appendicitis patient with aspirin for the pain and fever when the appropriate treatment is an appendectomy! Similarly, the task of the business case student is to identify the real problem and take appropriate action (not just treat symptoms).

More advanced classes may involve cases that capture the complexity of the business environment with no particular guidance as to how to approach the situation. For intermediate-level financial management courses, though, we focus on business problems associated specifically with financial management and narrow enough to be effective lessons, given your current and prior exposure to financial concepts and theories. The cases in this volume are appropriate for courses beyond the first financial management course. While we do not generally recommend their use at the graduate level, there may be occasions to use some of these cases to highlight lecture topics in lower-level masters courses. These cases can also serve masters-level courses designed to bring non-business undergraduates up to speed for graduate study in business.

What to Expect for Case Assignments

Finance professors differ with respect to how the case approach will be integrated into the course. Some will use cases as the major resource for a class, while others may integrate cases into the traditional mix of lectures, research assignments, and textbook readings. There is also substantial variation in professors' expectations from students in a case assignment, anywhere from preparation of the case for discussion in class, to complete analyses to be turned in or presented. The following is just a very general guideline as to how to approach the cases in this textbook.

Reading the Case

There is a technique to reading a case. While cases are used to expose you to financial situations, there is a distinct difference between financial reality and financial cases. In real situations, we must perceive problems and issues needy of attention. These are sometimes highlighted by conflicts, tensions, or crises. A financial case, on the other hand, is written because there is an issue worthy of development of a learning tool. In reading a case, you need to realize that the author of the case is implying that an issue exists, and that some requirement for action is anticipated. For cases in this book, you can expect that the information presented is usually sufficient for you to develop an understanding of the situation, without the distracting influences that are always present in the real world. In some of the cases, you will have to assess the necessity for assumptions, prudently applied. In the real world, facts and data are often background noise; information is usually available, but no one is there to tell us what is relevant and what is irrelevant (master's level cases often include much more information, in order to train the student to discern between noise and pertinent facts).

We recommend two readings of the case. On the first reading, approach the case as a story, looking for the plot and story development. Try to relate the facts to one another. Try to determine why the case was written, what lesson is intended, and what possible financial concepts and tools will be required to analyze the case. On the second reading, concentrate on the details of the case. Examine the data, and develop an understanding of the decision at hand. Take notes on the key items, and remember where you saw pertinent facts. Questions at the end of each case sometimes serve as a guide as to how to approach the analysis, but "doing the questions" does not substitute for an effective reading of the case.

Analyzing the Case

For each of these cases, questions guide you through the process of the learning experience. A particular case, though, can have a richer lesson, which your professor may want to explore. While analyzing a situation from a financial standpoint is important, it is also important for you to realize that the analysis takes place in a business environment, where many other concerns exist. For example, consider case number 11, Lehman Container Corporation. The case task is the financial analysis of the projects, but there exists some obvious problems with handling strong diverse opinions from opposing managers (exhibit 4). Unnecessary irritation of upper management may jeopardize an analyst's future employment! The financial analysis must sometimes be tempered with considerations that are non-financial in nature.

For focused cases such as these, it is important to properly apply financial management concepts and analysis techniques to the situation described in the case. Conclusions should be supported by the analysis. A former student who has become a wise financial manager has said, "Your opinion doesn't matter until you're the boss. Let your analysis do the talking." A complete and proper analysis often carries substantially more weight than an opinion, even for upper managers. Similarly, with case analyses professors often place greater importance on students' demonstration of mastery of financial concepts and tools rather than on their assertiveness in expressing unsupported opinions.

In this book, a variety of financial management topics are covered, providing for a breadth of experiential learning. It is our expressed desire that you will use this casebook to develop a better understanding of financial management than is possible using only conceptual and theoretical textbooks. Working cases can better prepare you as a finance practitioner and accelerate your entry into higher levels of managerial responsibility.

Acknowledgements

We would like to acknowledge the contributions of other authors on several of the cases in this volume:

E. Lee Makamson (Community Memorial Hospital)

P. Michael McLain (KHF Corporation, Bill Thurmond Pig Farm, Bentley Custom Ceramics)

Sean Brandon (NCI Corporation)

About the Authors

Dr. Robert Stretcher is a finance professor at Sam Houston State University. He has 21 years of teaching experience in finance. He is president of the Institute of Finance Case Research and Executive Editor of the *Journal of Finance Case Research*. Professor Stretcher is among the foremost scholars involved in case teaching and research, and has published numerous articles in these areas, as well as a wide variety of other finance areas. Professor Stretcher's PhD is in finance and monetary macroeconomic theory from the University of Tennessee.

Dr. Timothy B. Michael is a finance professor at the University of Houston - Clear Lake. He has 14 years of teaching experience in finance. He serves as the Managing Editor of the *Journal of Finance Case Research*. Professor Michael has served as a casewriting consultant for several published works. Professor Michael's PhD is from the University of South Carolina, where he received outstanding teaching accolades.

SECTION 1

FINANCIAL STATEMENT ANALYSIS

Case 1

KHF CORPORATION

SEEDS OF DISTRESS

Jim Layton, controller for Kitty (Hawk Food), Inc. (KHF) was under considerable stress as he walked toward the chief executive's office. Marshall Horne, the CEO, was not known to take bad news well. In his hands, Jim held two letters from food suppliers that threatened to cancel KHF's trade credit accounts. KHF had developed difficulties in cash flow such that their payments on the accounts had been late, at best. The suppliers provided normal trade terms to KHF, with a 2% discount for early payment (within 10 days), and a 30 day limit. No purchase limits had been placed on the firm.

KHF had depended heavily on trade credit for the recent expansion of its service area into the Outer Banks of North Carolina. Jim, of course, was ultimately responsible for the firm's financial condition and performance. He fully expected to get a strong reprimand from Horne.

Mr. Horne was a big, burly man, never really seen without a faded baseball cap on his head. Not the sort of look a CEO might be expected to have. He was rather eccentric, as well, which complicated Jim's interaction with him. Horne had taken the firm from being a small food supplier in Edenton, North Carolina, to a moderate size regional supplier for restaurants throughout the northeastern part of the state. Horne seemed to have a way of appealing to the "good ole' boy" restauranteur, a personality very prevalent in this part of the state. Horne always had a mind full of jokes to share. Recently, he had somehow convinced the shareholders to vote in a name change from "Swamp Foods" to "Kitty (Hawk Food)." To Jim, the new name was rather silly and he thought to himself that it might even hurt business to have such an absurd title. Horne, however, appeared to be able to promote the humor of the name, and really seemed to enjoy traveling from business to business, picking up new customers. He had been almost solely responsible for the new business recently acquired in Nag's Head, Kill Devil Hills, and Kitty Hawk.

The entry into the resort areas of the Outer Banks had both doubled the firm's sales and had increased the firm's dependence on trade credit to accomplish the growth. It had also introduced a large degree of seasonality in KHF's business, because the major restaurant activity on the Outer Banks catered to summer tourism. Although Jim had been hired as controller, he had inherited the operational management that Horne had abandoned in preference to cajoling with his good ole' boy 'business associates.' Jim's time had been flooded with the operational concerns generated by rapid growth.

Jim had been hired fresh out of business school. He had attended a large state university in the area, and had looked forward to applying what he had learned to his work. He liked the company, and the position for which he was hired, controller. He felt challenged with the amount of work he had taken on, even overwhelmed at times. He also knew there were problems needy of solutions. He had double-majored in accounting and finance. The operational tasks were not his strength but he had felt obligated to take them on.

THE MEETING WITH HORNE

Jim's anxiety increased as he approached Horne's office, a 2,000 square foot 'luxury playroom' at the rear of the warehouse. It resembled a billiards/bar room. Horne often held beer parties there during televised football games. Jim had been to only a couple of these gatherings, mainly to preserve his relationship with Horne, but preferred to avoid the venue.

It was only 9:00 am. Horne had not left for his regular rounds yet. Jim knocked on the door. "Come on!" called Horne. Jim opened the door and silently groaned. He had interrupted a game of pool with Tibbs, one of Horne's 'associates,' a customer.

"Hello, Mr. Horne," Jim said. "Sorry to bother you, but I need to discuss some things with you."

Horne replied "Come on in - grab a cue." Horne was obviously in no mood to discuss serious business.

"Well, I appreciate it, but I need to get back to the warehouse. I really need a few minutes of your time," Jim said.

Horne sniffed, miffed that Jim had forced the issue. "Alright, what's up?"

"I have some correspondence from some of our business contacts," said Jim. He was trying to avoid discussing the details in front of Tibbs, but Horne didn't stop the game. "It's rather pressing."

"Well spit it out!" said Horne, obviously getting more agitated. Jim hesitated. "Well?" nudged Horne.

Jim took a deep breath. "Our two biggest suppliers are threatening to cut us off" said Jim. Horne looked up suddenly. Tibbs looked shocked.

"And HOW did you get us into that?" roared Horne, trying to save face. "Lets' see," he said, snatching the letters from Jim. "I'll be right back," he said, looking back at Tibbs.

Outside the office, Horne scowled at Jim. "What are you thinking, saying that in front of a customer?"

"I tried to avoid it - I asked you to give me a few minutes," replied Jim.

Horne read the letters. "Isn't it your job to keep these things from happening? What did they teach you at that business school anyway? If you want something done right, you have to do it yourself. I'll go see these idiots today and set things straight. Cut me two checks for the balances."

Jim stood his ground. "Unfortunately, we haven't collected most of our customer accounts. We don't have enough in the account to cover even half of one of these" replied Jim. Both of them knew that Horne was supposed to collect accounts due as he made the rounds of his customers.

Horne smacked the letters in frustration. "Get back to work!" he yelled, and stomped back into his office. Jim knew he had angered Horne by mentioning collections, but he also was unwilling to shoulder all the blame.

RELATIONSHIPS WITH THE SUPPLIERS

KHF was not a significantly large customer to either supplier. It would be unlikely that KHF could convince them to make further concessions; already the accounts were more than 60 days old. It was possible to find other suppliers for similar products, but KHF would need trade credit to fund purchases. Given the firm's record of lateness and new suppliers' reliance on credit references, the chance of establishing effective new relationships was questionable.

Another concern was that, although other suppliers had similar products, they were seldom exactly the same. Jim knew that restaurant owners were sometimes very picky about the character of the food they served. Last year, one of the popular products that KHF supplied, breaded chicken tenders, was replaced with a similar product, which had a different texture and flavor in the breading. The severity of the outcry from restaurant owners forced KHF into an emergency search for the prior product. KHF ended up buying the tenders directly from the producer, and restored the restaurant owners' confidence.

The relationships with the other suppliers was considerably less strained. KHF had been able to pay within the 30-day limits, albeit usually on day 30. The firm's other short-term creditors, two local bankers, were aware of KHF's cashflow problems, but had not pulled credit availability. This was probably because of Horne's relationships with each of the bankers. All of them had been boyhood friends. The two complaining suppliers, though, supplied roughly 65% of KHF's food supplies. They also had products that were unavailable elsewhere or substantially more expensive if ordered from other suppliers.

KHF had not had much difficulty in collecting most of the firm's accounts. The biggest problem came in the fall, when some of the resort restaurants simply closed and it was difficult to find the owners to collect any balances. Although there was a substantial period of time before payment was received (sometimes beyond the deadline), the number of bad accounts had not been problematic.

DISTRIBUTION OF BUSINESS

KHF's customers varied in size from small, individual restaurants to chain establishments having several restaurants within KHF's distribution area. The region had been broken down into six segments. The firm's more traditional segments were Edenton, Elizabeth City, and Williamston. The newer segments were Kitty Hawk, Kill Devil Hills, and Nags Head, all in the resort areas of the Outer Banks.

Although KHF did not carry all of the food products the restaurants needed, most of the basic needs were met. KHF did not carry fresh seafood, for example, which was in high demand by the restaurants, especially the ones on the Outer Banks. Basic items, however, like dry recipe ingredients (flour, sugar, etc.), canned items (fruits, vegetables), fresh produce and frozen and fresh meats (other than seafood) were provided by KHF. Except for seafood items, KHF was able to become the major supplier for most of the restaurants.

Within the past two years, though, some of the regional and national chain restaurants had opened at locations in KHF's service area. These restaurants had central buying, and Horne had found that they were only interested in fresh produce from local vendors. Horne preferred dealing with smaller chains and individual restauranteurs anyway, so he had abandoned marketing to the large chain restaurants.

In terms of total sales, each of the segments comprised the following percentages for the past year:

Service Segment	% of Total Sales
Edenton	18%
Elizabeth City	21%
Williamston	8%
Kitty Hawk	22%
Kill Devil Hills	15%
Nags Head	16%

THE NEXT STEPS

Jim silently walked back to his office in the front of the warehouse. He knew that Horne would soon come storming through on his way out. Jim definitely wanted to avoid additional conflict today, if possible. He decided that he needed to look physically busy until Horne left, then he would go about the task of figuring out how these problems had arisen, what the company's situation was, and how to go about solving it. He knew that Horne would complicate matters. Hopefully, Horne would wait to talk to the creditors and just go through his regular circuit of visiting his buddies for today.

REQUIRED:

1. Look at a map of Eastern North Carolina. Which of the towns served by KHF are resort areas? What proportion of KHF's business is resort business?

2. What are the characteristics of resort business in comparison to year-round business? Assuming these areas open for business around March 15th, and close around October 15th, would you say that KHF's overall business is seasonal?

3. Survey the financial condition and performance indicated by KHF's financial statements, and summarize your findings. Does anything stand out?

4. KHF is basically a merchandising firm, buying inventory, marking it up, and then selling it. Is KHF's dependence on trade accounts (both receivables and payables) surprising for a merchandising firm?

5. Develop a plan for solving KHF's problem.

Exhibit 1. KHF Income Statements. March 31, 2002 and March 31, 2003.

	2003	2002
NET SALES	$10,315,881	$9,474,409
Cost of Goods Sold	8,489,024	7,757,539
GROSS MARGIN	1,826,857	1,716,870
Operating and Other Expenses:		
Operating Expenses	-1,813,035	-1,747,097
Gain on Disposal	4,700	1,500
Rebates, Other Income	12,342	3,243
	-$1,795,993	-$1,742,354
INCOME FROM OPERATIONS	30,864	-25,484
Income Tax Expense	-8,440	7,089
NET INCOME	$22,424	-$18,395

Exhibit 2. KHF Balance Sheets. March 31, 2002 and March 31, 2003.

	2003	2002
ASSETS:		
Cash	$95,079	$41,488
Accounts Receivable	544,809	463,894
Inventory (LIFO)	442,588	480,950
Refundable Taxes		9,189
TOTAL CURRENT ASSETS	1,082,476	995,521
Property, Plant, and Equipment	1,453,611	1,292,417
less: Accumulated		
Depreciation	-876,784	-770,988
Net PPE	576,827	521,429
Other Assets	23,836	19,581
TOTAL ASSETS	1,683,139	1,536,531
LIABILITIES:		
Notes payable- Current	148,832	119,489
Accounts payable	824,447	674,936
Accrued Expenses	12,298	16,560
Taxes Payable	13,223	10,582
TOTAL CURRENT LIABILITIES	998,800	821,567
Long Term Liabilities	185,084	238,133
TOTAL LIABILITIES	1,183,884	1,059,700
EQUITY:		
Common Stock	100,000	100,000
Retained Earnings	399,255	376,831
TOTAL EQUITY	499,255	476,831
TOTAL LIABILITIES AND		
EQUITY	$1,683,139	$1,536,531

Case 2

COMMUNITY GENERAL HOSPITAL

Dr. Noland Wright*, newly appointed manager of Community General Hospital, sighed as he reviewed the hospital's financial records. He had been given the responsibility of leading the hospital's next steps, but was perplexed by the financial condition highlighted in the financial statements before him. His training was in medicine, not business, and he had recently taken early retirement. He had been talked into taking Community's reins by some old friends who lived a few miles away from the facility.

Community General Hospital had initially begun in 1914 as Whittaker Memorial Hospital, a community-run hospital serving the black population of Newport News, Virginia. To meet the needs of an economic expansion of the community largely due to increased commercial activity during World War II, the hospital expanded facilities and scope through federal funding. In the 1940's the hospital increased its census and gained accreditation by the American College of Surgeons. In the 1950's and 60's the hospital enjoyed a bustling business in the segregated health care industry.

With the advent of the desegregation movement in the 1960's, the hospital experienced several threats as black physicians gained the ability to admit patients to the large and better equipped traditionally 'white' hospitals in the area. The civic organization that governed the hospital began to be concerned for the hospital's survival. It was experiencing a falling census, a deteriorating reputation concerning the quality of its health care, and picked up the reputation of being a 'public' hospital (which it was not). While the City of Newport News was willing to help, it was unwilling to acquire full responsibility for the costs of a public hospital. During the 1970's, the hospital drew on an emergency fund set up by the city.

Throughout the 1970's, the hospital suffered from losses and bad debts. By 1982 the civic board that guided the hospital became inactive. The following year, the last of the segregation practices ended by court order at the large surrounding hospitals. Few patients desired to be admitted to the small, modestly equipped hospital, preferring the large, modern hospitals they now had access to. The hospital ended 1983 with a $402,000 budget deficit. Suppliers began demanding cash payments for purchases. Employee layoffs, tightening of admission criteria, and refusal of non-paying patients were some of the steps taken to alleviate the dire financial situation. It was hoped that a new facility, new location and a future change of name to Community General Hospital would help the hospital to survive. A $15 million bond issue and $1.5 million in community pledges allowed the hospital to continue to operate. At the end of 1984 the fund deficit was $749,000. Private healthcare management firms were solicited for help, but these efforts were short-lived.

In July 1985, Community General Hospital was dedicated, with a new facility and equipment, and a higher occupancy rate. Between 1979 and 1985, seven different administrators had been in charge of the hospital. Continued losses after 1985, and continued difficulty in retaining continuous management, convinced the hospital's supporters to seek some solution to the ongoing problems. Political avenues were tried with some success, but did not last. The sale of the hospital to a doctors' investment group was considered, but the hospital's supporters ultimately rejected the deal.

By 1990 the debt was in excess of $20 million. The 'board' of supporters agreed to file for bankruptcy. The Guarantor of the mortgage, the U.S. Department of Housing and Urban Development, took over the mortgage debt. The hospital continued to operate as the board sought affiliations with other area hospitals. The quality ratings for the hospital continued to suffer. In 1993 the hospital was granted its bankruptcy petition. HUD settled for $4 million, and other creditors were held at bay.

Political solutions for Community General's future were sought, but ultimately, did not help the hospital's condition. Administrators were hired, but their tenures were short-lived. By mid 1996 the hospital was again running a large fund deficit and was seeking direction in what appeared to be a rather hopeless situation.

The financial statements for Community General Hospital appear in Exhibits 1-4.

REQUIRED

1. With a quick observation of Community General Hospital's financial statements, what can one conclude concerning a) profitability (nonprofit viability), solvency, and cash flow?

2. What are the root causes of the current condition of the hospital?

3. Come up with some alternative solutions for Community General Hospital. According to your recommendations, is Dr. Wright the man for the job?

4. Select one (or a combination) of the alternatives you propose. Illustrate the necessary steps involved with your plan's implementation, especially concerning funding sources for implementation of your recommendation(s), and concerning repayment of debt.

Exhibit 1. Income Statement for the years ended June 30, 1994, and June 30, 1995.

	1994	1995
OPERATING REVENUE		
Net Patient Revenue	$8,528,383	$9,858,446
Other	386,285	253,563
TOTAL	$8,914,668	$10,112,009
OPERATING EXPENSES		
	3,355,391	3,540,940
Payroll Taxes	1,026,076	1,274,260
Physician Fees	807,431	787,895
Contracted Services	1,581,970	1,564,821
Medical Supplies	738,677	782,988
General Supplies	165,038	171,957
Utilities	319,613	279,288
Insurance	128,486	163,558
Legal	52,458	66,508
Rental	142,229	119,594
Other	197,854	170,065
Bad Debt	278,389	544,602
TOTAL OPERATING EXP.	$8,793,612	$9,466,476
INCOME(LOSS) BEFORE INTEREST AND DEPRECIATION	$121,056	$645,533
NONOPERATING LOSSES		
Interest	33,554	105,325
Depreciation	802,490	771,492
Reorganization Cost	72,458	0
TOTAL NONOPERATING LOSSES	$908,502	$876,817
INCOME OR LOSS BEFORE NONRECURRING BAD-DEBT WRITEOFF	-$787,446	-$231,284
NONRECURRING BAD-DEBT WRITEOFF	$0	$439,720
EXPENSES AND LOSSES IN EXCESS OF REVENUES AND GAINS	-$787,446	-$671,004

Exhibit 2. Balance Sheet. June 30, 1994, and June 30, 1995.

	1994	1995
ASSETS		
CURRENT ASSETS		
Cash	$791,893	$577,461
Trade Receivables	1,539,390	2,062,142
Other Receivables	7,847	46,449
Supplies Inventory	271,997	277,191
Prepaid Expenses	85,265	102,066
TOTAL CURRENT ASSETS	$2,696,392	$3,065,309
PROPERTY AND EQUIPMENT		
Land	276,865	276,864
Buildings	8,772,782	8,772,782
Equipment and Fixtures	5,243,738	5,354,421
TOTAL	$14,293,385	$14,404,067
Accumulated Depreciation	6,999,531	7,535,929
NET PROPERTY AND EQUIPMENT	$7,293,854	$6,868,138
OTHER ASSETS		
Deposits	87,113	87,113
Unamortized Debt Expense	522,850	522,850
TOTAL OTHER ASSETS	$609,963	$609,963
TOTAL ASSETS	$10,600,209	$10,543,410
LIABILITIES		
CURRENT LIABILITIES		
Accounts Payable	$802,184	$1,036,151
Notes Payable	0	40,000
Due to 3rd Party Payors	2,924,863	2,840,027
Accrued Payroll	59,569	58,926
Accrued Vacation	192,881	251,500
Other Accrued Expenses	498,133	312,049
TOTAL CURRENT LIABILITIES	$4,477,630	$4,538,653
LONG TERM LIABILITIES		
Capital Lease	0	29,317
LIABILITIES SUBJECT TO COMPROMISE	21,972,071	21,972,071
TOTAL LIABILITIES	26,449,701	26,540,041
FUND DEFICIT	-15,849,492	-15,996,631
TOTAL LIABILITIES + FUND DEFICIT	$10,600,209	$10,543,410

Exhibit 3. Statement of Cash Flows for the years ended June 30, 1994, and June 30, 1995

	1994	1995
CASH FLOWS FROM OPERATING ACTIVITIES, GAINS, AND LOSSES:		
Expenses and Losses in Excess of Revenues and Gains	-$787,436	-$671,004
Adjustments: Operating Activities:		
Depreciation and Amortization	802,490	771,492
Increase in Accounts Receivable	-579,126	-561,354
Increase in Inventories	8,819	-5,194
Increase in Prepaid Expenses	23,016	-16,801
Increase in Other Assets	-10,000	0
Increase in Accounts Payable	414,591	233,967
Decrease in Third Party Payable	1,041,761	-84,836
Decrease in Accrued Expenses	-161,185	-128,108
	$1,540,366	$209,166
NET CASH PROVIDED FROM OPERATING ACTIVITIES, GAINS AND LOSSES	$752,930	-$461,838
CASH FLOWS FROM INVESTING ACTIVITIES:		
Purchase of Property and Equipment	-154,944	-55,258
NET CASH USED: INVESTING ACTIVITIES	-$154,944	-$55,258
CASH FLOWS FROM FINANCING ACTIVITIES:		
Principal Payments on Capital Lease	0	-26,107
Net Borrowing on Line of Credit	0	40,000
NET CASH USED: FINANCING ACTIVITIES	$0	$13,893
NET INCREASE: CASH AND EQUIVALENTS	$597,986	-$503,203
PRIOR PERIOD ADJUSTMENT	$0	$288,771
CASH AND EQUIVALENTS AT BEGINNING OF YEAR	$193,907	$791,893
CASH AND CASH EQUIVALENTS AT END OF YEAR	$791,893	$577,461

Exhibit 4. Statement of Fund Surplus (Deficit) for the years ended June 30, 1994, and June 30, 1995

FUND DEFICIT: July 1, 1993	-$15,062,056
Expenses and Losses in Excess of Revenues and Gains	-787,436
FUND DEFICIT: June 30, 1994	-15,849,492
Expenses and Losses in Excess of Revenues and Gains	-671,004
FUND DEFICIT: June 30, 1995	-$16,520,496

REFERENCES

American Hospital Association. The AHA Guide. Chicago, Illinois: AHA.

Daily Press, "NN General Leader Under Attack." August 27, 1995.

Daily Press, "Special Report: Newport News General Hospital." March 7, 1993.

Rice, Mitchell F. and Jones, Woodrow, Jr. Public Policy and the Black Hospital: From Slavery to Segregation to Integration. Westport, Connecticut: Greenwood Press 1990.

Virginia Health Services Cost Review Council.

Special recognition should be given to E. Lee Makamson, who did background research on Newport News General Hospital (the subject company), and was the principal co-author of a comprehensive strategic version of this case (Hampton University School of Business Working Paper #WP 1997-05, March 13, 1997). This version is adopted from the original working paper.

*Dr. Noland Wright is a fictitious name, and is placed in a fictitious role as the newly hired manager of Community General Hospital. No similarity to real persons is implied or intended. Details about the condition of the organization are factual.

Case 3

BILL THURMOND PIG FARM

Walt Thurmond put down the latest newsletter on market prices for local agricultural products. He hated to approach his Dad, Bill Thurmond, about the current conditions. Bill Thurmond Pig Farm had been in the family for three generations of "Bill's" and one generation of "Walt" Thurmond. The Thurmonds had always managed, somehow, to ride out the tough periods in the past. Walt had been following the markets, though, and had come to the realization that market prices were approaching a level where it may not even be worth keeping their livestock, much less delivering them to market.

Over the years, Bill and Walt had developed a productive breeding stock of boars and sows; so productive, in fact, that it had almost become a problem to keep their herd within manageable proportions. In the past few years, neighboring farmers had no need for any extras, and in 1995 and 1996, the Thurmonds had transported record numbers of top-hogs to market.

Walt had taken over the business three years prior, when the farm's success had convinced Bill to semi-retire, leaving to Walt most of the decision making. Walt had dreams of being in the same position one day, leaving the farm to his son, now five years old. The two had set up the farm in a corporate structure to make transitions of ownership easier. At the same time, the name was changed to Thurmond Farms, Inc. Although the net income result was not great, the business did support the family through salaries.

Walt certainly didn't want his Dad to think that he had taken over the business and failed. It wasn't that the expenses of the farm had been allowed to creep up; Walt had done a fair job of keeping the expenses at a reasonable level. The only threat to cost control for the farm were some new environmental regulations affecting hog waste. Walt had no idea the extent to which these requirements would increase his cost. Market demand had not been decreasing drastically, but hog prices just were simply not staying up. Walt had cut livestock inventory some, and was selling fewer and fewer hogs as time passed, since prices were so low. Unfortunately, that meant he still had to feed the hogs he had decided not to sell.

Walt had earlier taken the position that continued production was probably not harmful to the farm. He had invested most of the cash flow back into the business at the beginning of the year, so although the asset base of the farm was relatively large, most of the assets were

17

productive assets and not easily convertible into cash. The farm was poised for a large market run, but prices were discouraging that.

The farm did have quite a bit of timber that Walt could sell to raise some liquidity, but timber harvest was at the bidding of timber buyers and there was no guarantee as to when they might want to harvest. Selling the timber rights was a possibility, as well. The drawback there was that the agreement held until harvesting occurred, and only then was payment received, no matter how long the timber company wanted to wait. If worse came to worse, Walt could sell parts of the farm that had highway frontage, which would diminish the farm's total acreage only slightly, but would bring fairly high prices. He knew of several people who would jump at the chance to buy the parcels at fair prices.

Walt's line of thought was interrupted suddenly. Buck, the family's pet border collie, was announcing the arrival of Bill's truck. Walt saw the headlights approaching the house as he got up from his chair. "Well," he thought to himself, "Now's as good a time as any to break the news."

Walt met his Dad on the front porch. "Have you heard the market news?" Bill asked.

In a way, Walt was relieved that Bill had asked, and that perhaps he had been mulling it over already. "Yes, I just read the Northeastern North Carolina farmers' newsletter. Robinson and Morehead got cash prices of only eight cents a pound on their last shipments. They're considering selling the rest of their pigs in the Midwest somewhere - the prices are higher there." The two farmers mentioned in the newsletter were neighboring farmers who were also dependent on cash pricing.

Bill's countenance suddenly changed. "Oh. Well, take a look at this," Bill said. He handed Walt a USDA publication showing average prices for the entire United States. Walt groaned. The last price on the nationwide data was only eighteen cents a pound. "Those numbers include contract prices for the big farms. Market prices are even worse than those numbers, I'm sure." Bill said. "I doubt Robinson and Morehead can do much better on cash prices in the Midwest. Plus, they will spend a lot of money to get their hogs there."

Walt was perplexed. He had never had to deal with such low prices. True, hog prices tended to fluctuate rather wildly, and had been down to the low 30's and high 20's before, but never this low. Additionally, Walt had streamlined the farm to be more productive and had trimmed many of the unnecessary costs. Under normal circumstances that would be good, because there was more livestock (currently about 5,000 pigs) to sell and the costs were lower. No amount of cost cutting he had done in the past two years, however, could make up for such low prices at market. Walt now had very little cash and a bumper crop of pigs. He had sold only 118 pigs so far in 1998.

"Walt, maybe you need to drive up to Smithfield and have a talk with Jackson. The Christmas season is coming up, and they always need extra stock," Bill said. Walt had basically two customers, both local packers. Bud Jackson was the buyer for one of them, a large producer of packaged ham in Virginia. The other one was a national brand packer that bought mostly on contract from the large farms, but had always been interested in Walt's livestock for cash sales.

"Maybe we should have tried to make some contracts a few years ago when we had the chance," Bill mused. "At the time, I guess I was enjoying getting so much more than the contract suppliers were getting."

"Not a very good time to lock in a contract, though, Dad," Walt replied. "I'll go and see Bud tomorrow. We obviously can't afford to auction this herd at the market at those prices."

Walt sat silently on the porch for a few moments. "Dad, what have you done in the past when it gets like this? I mean, we've had hard times before, right?"

"Never really had to deal with this particular situation, son," Bill responded. "You know as well as I do that prices don't go down and stay there for long. It's just a question of when they turn.

MARKET AND FINANCIAL INFORMATION

Thurmond Farms financial records are presented in Exhibit 1. The income statement for 1998 is a year to date summary through the 18th of November, 1998. Exhibit 2 is the USDA report referred to earlier in the case.

Exhibit 1. Profit and Loss Statements, 1995 to 1998.

	1995	1996	1997	1998*
Sales of livestock	$1,099,120	$660,880	$375,000	$104,750
Cooperative Distributions	10,760	11,070	7,950	5,500
Agricultural Payments	15,360	0	0	0
Total Revenue	$1,125,240	$671,950	$382,950	$110,250
Custom Hire	$12,500	$11,190	$20,000	$0
Salaries & Compensation	$92,000	$98,000	$102,000	$84,000
Depreciation	293,490	112,390	89,370	47,300
Feed Purchased	273,800	448,290	126,250	42,440
Fertilizers and Lime	6,140	0	0	0
Insurance	41,720	34,670	23,350	22,380
Mortgage Interest	88,590	35,710	24,070	11,660
Rent-Machinery	14,710	0	0	0
Repairs and Maint	28,960	24,500	7,730	0
Seeds and plants	13,840	0	0	0
Supplies	62,410	29,380	31,050	45,230
Taxes	17,900	10,510	11,580	10,730
Utilities	50,850	54,580	15,450	24,550
Other	44,710	68,020	26,370	11,470
Total Expenses	$1,041,620	$927,240	$477,220	$299,760
Profit/Loss	$83,620	-$255,290	-$94,270	-$189,510
Pigs Sold	12,080	10,110	4,740	1,180
Average Weight (lbs)	332	322	354	355

*1998 to Nov 18

Exhibit 2: Hog Prices Per Pound Received by Farmers, USA (cents)
(Source: USDA)

YEAR	JAN	FEB	MAR	APR	MAY	JUN	JUL	AUG	SEP	OCT	NOV	DEC	AVG
1993	41.2	44	46.5	45.4	46.9	48.1	45.7	47.3	47.8	46.9	42.5	38.6	45.2
1994	43.5	47.9	44.4	42.7	42.7	42.7	42.2	41.8	35.4	31.8	28	41.7	39.9
1995	36.8	39.1	37.8	35.6	37.1	42.2	46.3	48.6	48.4	45.7	39.9	40.4	40.5
1996	42.6	46.5	48.7	49.7	56.8	56.4	58.6	59.7	54.7	55.6	54.4	30.9	51.9
1997	53.8	52.8	49.4	53.8	58.2	57.8	58.9	55.3	50.4	47.3	45.1	43.5	52.9
1998	36	35.9	34.9	35.6	42.3	42.4	36.9	35.2	29.5	27.8	18.8		

Transportation Costs to Market: $.05 per pound
Maintenance & feeding of Herd: $.03 per pound per month

WALT'S DILEMMA

Walt knew he had to make some decision about what to do with the herd. He walked past the main corral. The hogs were healthy and large. The thought of killing and burying them seemed revolting to Walt, yet several of the neighboring farmers had done just that, because they could not keep feeding herds that had so little chance of covering those costs with market prices as low as they were. The big question was whether or not to continue maintaining the herd in hopes of getting substantially higher prices in the near future. Walt was also somewhat perturbed at the buyers that the prices had to crash just when the quality and quantity of his pigs had taken such a favorable turn. The farm had become more efficient and more productive over the two year term.

His mind wandered to a line in the movie "Gone with the Wind" when Scarlet O'Hara says "I don't want to think about that today; I'll think about that tomorrow." He decided not to decide yet. A good night's sleep certainly wouldn't hurt, and the problem would still be waiting in the morning.

REQUIRED

1. According to financial principles, what would you recommend to Walt?

2. The Thurmond farm is located on high ground, never really susceptible to flooding. Why did this fact become extremely positive for the Thurmonds in September 1999?

SECTION 2

TIME VALUE AND VALUATION

CASE 4

RETIREMENT PLANNING:
ROBERT AND LINDA TRUDEAU

"Here it is!" Linda yelled. Her husband, Robert, was upstairs in the bedroom. "Here what is?" he asked back. "The summary for your 401K plan," Linda replied.

Robert and Linda Trudeau had, for some time, been collecting account summaries from their various investments, and having appraisals done on their real estate and valuables. Ron Lamont, their financial advisor, had suggested that they do this, since they were considering retiring in several years. Ron, a member of their church and a family friend, had presented a financial planning seminar on three weeknights at the church. Ron had presented the seminar many times at other churches, as well. While Ron had agreed to informally advise them, he had refused any compensation for doing so. "It's a ministry," he would say when the Trudeaus had offered to pay him.

The 401k information had been slow in coming, and was the last bit of information the Trudeaus needed to complete their financial summary for Ron's examination.

BACKGROUND

Robert and Linda had been married for twenty-eight years. They had raised two children, Pamela and Janet, who had graduated college and were out on their own. Pam was married, and Jan was pursuing a career as a paralegal. It was safe to say that Pam and Jan were not in any way financially dependent on their parents. They had both learned at an early age to save for desired items, and Robert and Linda had promoted that lesson by providing "bonus dollars" if the girls saved their money for certain purposes. For example, any money saved for spending at college was matched dollar for dollar by Robert and Linda, and saving for a car received 20% matching.

Ever since their girls had 'left the nest,' Robert and Linda had gone about serious investment with their eventual retirement in mind. They had saved about twenty percent of their income for two years, and had restructured some of their investments to try to gain some ground toward an acceptable asset level. Gathering all of the information for Ron had taken them almost four months. It was surprising how many different accounts they had used to store wealth!

THE MEETING WITH RON

Robert had scheduled a meeting with Ron to present their information and come up with a plan as to how to reach their retirement goals. The doorbell rang as they were clearing the dining room table for the work.

Linda answered the door. "Hi. Ron! Thank you for coming" Linda said as Ron came in the door.

"No problem," Ron Replied. "Glad to help out."

"I got you a BIG cup of coffee," Robert said as he placed the tray down on the table, There were three jumbo cups, resembling bowls more than cups. "We may be here for a while."

"Well, why don't we get started," Ron replied. "How old are you guys, anyway?"

Linda looked startled. "I guess you have to know all of that, don't you? We are both 54 years old. We figure we have thirteen more years to work, if we retire at the normal age, 67. But we were wondering if it would be financially possible for us to retire early? We'd kind of like to have a few years where we're still young enough to enjoy traveling and doing some things we have always wanted to."

Ron sipped his coffee. "Well, that all depends on the date of retirement, the amount of wealth you can accumulate until then, and the amount of wealth you have accumulated so far. Do you have all of your account balances and yields, and your appraisal items?"

"Yes, they're all here," Robert replied as he brought the shoebox of statements and appraisals over to the table.

"The first thing we need to do is to list each account, what type it is, and what characteristics each one has," Ron said. "We need to list the current balance, and the return it is expected to earn for the forseeable future. Given your time horizon, we need to assess where changes may need to be made."

Linda spoke up, "How do we know what to keep and what to cash in?" she asked.

Ron thought for a second. "Lets deal with two scenarios, just to keep it simple. Suppose you have two choices; either to retire in thirteen years, at age 67 and a half, or retire early, say at age 60. You both remember the big dip in the stock market in 2000 and 2001?"

Robert and Linda both nodded. "Our aggressive growth stock fund lost over two-thirds of its value," Robert replied.

"Exactly" Ron said, "You don't want that to happen again right before you plan to stop working. As you get nearer the time to retire, you will probably want to cash in that stock fund at opportune times and place the funds in safer investments. Now you know, the long term return will probably be less, but you no longer have the long term to play with! As you near retirement, you will want to make sure and preserve the wealth, hopefully at a decent return. If you're going to retire at age 60, you probably should do that at least five years ahead of time. Of course, if you have some money you'd like to leave in the stock account, and you can still bear the risk of stock funds, you could do that. The bulk of your wealth, though, you need to protect. If you're going to retire at age 67 1/2, start liquidating your riskier accounts at age 62. Tell you what. Let's list all of your assets and we'll put an asterisk by the ones that are riskier. These you should target for liquidation five years ahead of retirement. Then we'll write out to the side where the funds should go."

"I'd really like to get them taken care of now, not just before retirement," Robert said. "The return isn't as important as preserving the amount we've saved so far. Let's just decide where everything goes, and do it as soon as we can get it done."

"That's fine; we'll go with that plan," Ron replied. "Let's add a column on the right of each line, called 'action,' that indicates what to do with each account."

"Should we keep on contributing to the accounts we're putting money in every month?" Linda asked.

"Lets list them separately, Linda, and we'll deal with each one individually," Ron replied.

Robert pulled four account summaries from the pile. "These are the ones we are currently contributing to," Robert said.

"Good!" said Ron. "Lets list out the monthly contribution to each one; you both receive paychecks monthly, right?"

"Correct," Linda replied.

"We'll total your monthly contributions, and decide what to continue to invest those in," Ron said. "We'll summarize accounts currently contributed to monthly as exhibit one, and the accounts you are not contributing to every month as exhibit two," Ron said. "Do you have any real estate assets, valuable personal property, or other types of assets you would want to use for retirement income?" Ron asked.

"Yes, I would like to sell that ugly painting in the living room - I never have liked it," Linda replied. "I also have about $5,500 of jewelry that I really don't wear, and we have a firm offer from our jeweler for that price. Other than that, there's the rental house, but we might keep that. Real estate investments are good, aren't they?"

Ron frowned. "That all depends," he said. "Does the property give you any grief? he asked.

"Yes it does," Robert exclaimed. "But I must admit, it does return some good cashflow to us every month."

"Oh, you have had it rented constantly?" Ron asked.

"No, it is typically rented about ten months out of each year on average." Robert thought further and said "In fact, we have had to do a lot of work on it recently. It needed a new water heater, new carpeting, painting, and furnace this last time we had a tenant move out. Cost me a fortune!"

"OK, folks. It sounds like we need to determine the actual return on the rental house, and then you can decide whether it is worth the grief or not. Rentals can sometimes be good, but most of the ones people tell me about are more trouble than they are worth. If you have it as kind of a hobby, that's one thing, but if you look at it as strictly an investment, that is totally different."

"I don't consider it a hobby. Let's evaluate it strictly based on the return. I could sell it tomorrow, if that's what we need to do," Robert said.

"Well, let's see," Ron said. "The total return, after your expenses, will be about four and a half percent."

"We'll sell it," Robert concluded.

"Some friends of ours invested their savings in an account that basically provides them with a guaranteed interest payment every month," Linda said. "It amounts to .58 percent per month on the balance, which is constant. They want to leave the balance to their children when they die. Can we do the same thing?"

"Yes, but I will suggest one revision. It's kind of risky to rely on a single account held with a single annuity company for your retirement income. I suggest splitting your money into maybe four accounts. That way, if something happens to one, your entire income won't be affected, only the part from that one account. Most of these plans are insured, but sometimes you can miss a few checks before problems are resolved."

"Good idea," Robert and Linda both replied at once.

"I'd like to keep our growth fund, though, even after retirement," Robert said. "It has had a great return, even if you include the 2000-2001 period. I'm just going to leave it alone and let it grow, just as a safety net. We won't plan on taking any income from it before or after retirement."

"You can definitely do that, Robert. I think a safety net is good. An account like that usually experiences some pretty wild upswings and downswings, so it's good not to rely on it for income," reflected Ron. "Many people did that in the 90's and suffered greatly in the downturn. What you're proposing is a much better way to use it."

Robert, Linda, and Ron summarized all of the information into Exhibits one through five.

"You can plan on funneling the balances for these accounts into the annuity accounts on your retirement date, except for the growth account, which you have indicated you want to be separate. You'll keep the vehicles and your home, I take it?"

"Yes, that's right," Linda replied.

"Well, let me take this to the office and I'll get back to you at the end of the week," Ron said.

"You sure we can't pay you something for your services?" Robert asked.

"No, no, none of that," Ron replied, and with that, he departed.

Exhibit 1. Accounts Receiving New Investment Every Month.

Type of Account	Monthly Contribution	Current Balance	Average Return	Compound Frequency	Action
Joint IRA	300	$84,203	5.9%	monthly	keep
Online Broker	200	$56,909	10.3%	monthly	to CD's*
Robert TSA	560	$343,039	9%	monthly	to Index Fund TSA*
Bond Fund	$110	$29,937	5.5%	Monthly	keep

*Same $560 payment into Index Fund TSA plus $200 that used to go to the online brokerage account

Exhibit 2. Account Balances: No New Investment.

Type of Account	Current Balance	Average Return	Compound Frequency	Action
Savings	$4,200	1.8%	quarterly	keep
Bank CD's	9,980	3.4%	semiannual	keep
Growth fund	313,092	11%	monthly	to Index Fund
Income fund	19,376	6.5%	monthly	keep
Money mkt	11,933	3.8%	daily	keep

Exhibit 3. Real Estate and Personal Property Asset Values.

Type of Asset	Current Value	Action
Home	$282,000	keep
Rental Home	$151,000	sell, pay off home mortgage, rest to new 7.5% utilities stock fund
Painting	$18,000	sell, to money mkt
Jewelry	$5,500	sell, to money mkt
Automobiles	$94,000	keep

Exhibit 4. Other Balances.

Type of Account	Current Balance	Average Return	Compound Frequency	Action
CU Savings	$4,304	1.8%	quarterly	liquidate, to money mkt

Exhibit 5. Debt Balances.

Type of Account	Current Balance	Compound Frequency	Action
Home Mortgage	$124,200	monthly	pay off

Exhibit 6. Asset Descriptions

Joint IRA: Individual Retirement Account owned jointly by Robert and Linda
Online Broker: Stock shares held in an online brokerage account
Robert TSA: Tax Sheltered Annuity plan through Robert's employer
Bond Fund: Shares in a mutual fund that invests in bonds
Savings: A savings account at the Trudeau's bank
Bank CD's: Certificates of deposit held at the Trudeau's bank
Growth fund: Shares in a mutual fund that invests in growth stocks
Income fund: Shares in a mutual fund that invests in high-payout stocks
Money mkt: Shares in an investment fund that invests in money market instruments
Home: The Trudeau's primary residence
Rental Home: A duplex about four miles from the Trudeau's home
Painting: The ugly painting Linda doesn't like
Jewelry: The jewelry that Linda intends to sell
Automobiles: The Trudeau's two cars
CU Savings: A savings account at a credit union in town
Home Mortgage: The balance owed on the Trudeau's home loan
Index Fund: Shares in a mutual fund that invests in stocks in a published index, like the S&P 500 (6.9%, monthly)
Index Fund TSA: Same as above, but tax sheltered (11.1%, monthly)

REQUIRED

1. Carry out the transactions indicated in the "action" columns for each account, and create a table (using the exhibit format as a guide) for the surviving accounts.

2. If the Trudeaus retire at age 60, how much wealth will they have built up, given the strategy outlined in exhibit 4? What if they retire at age 67 1/2? For simplicity, all returns listed are already adjusted for taxes (they are aftertax returns).

3. The Trudeaus estimate that they could live on $10,000 per month after retiring, taking into account the fact that inflation may occur. They have already adjusted their estimated need according to that inflation expectation. Assuming this dollar amount will not change, and that the Trudeaus will live until age 85, is their savings adequate to retire at age 60? At age 67 1/2?

4. According to good financial planning principles, how would you recommend making up for the difference between what they have and what they desire as an annuity after retirement? How much extra do they need to save in that account per month?

5. Should they consider retiring at age 60 or not? Justify your answer.

CASE 5

PEARSON CORPORATION

Pearson Corporation is a producer of customizing accessories for automobiles located in Charlotte, North Carolina. The company is relatively new, only in business since 1998. John Pearson, the owner and general manager, started the company with funds from an inheritance. John was only 19 years old in 1998. He 'blew' his inheritance on manufacturing equipment that he used to mold plastics and fabricate metal products. He used these as inputs for final products which, according to John, were custom touches he would be "drooling over for his own car."

BACKGROUND

John had long been an enthusiast over chrome replacement parts, sound systems, and body enhancements since he bought his first car in 1994. His car was very modest at first, but had gained the reputation of 'coolness' by the time he had customized it. John also acquired an uncanny ability to convince others to follow his design ideas. All of his friends customized their own cars according to his modifications on his car, and the fever had spread to the community and the entire state before long. John was always at gatherings of young people showing off their custom cars, anywhere from the local Wal-Mart parking lot to formal shows sponsored by custom parts manufacturers.

John always wanted to be able to make his living by designing and selling custom products of his own, but never could pass off the thought as anything more than a 'boyhood folly,' as his mother put it. She much preferred that he go to college and get an education that would get him a steady paycheck after graduation. Their opposed ideas continued until John's grandmother passed away in 1996, leaving him almost $125,000 in cash, tax free. John immediately hired an attorney and a CPA to set up a company for him and to handle the transactions summaries and legal aspects of the business. He learned how to fabricate plastic and metal components, and designed several customizing add-ons. His first products hit the local parts stores in 1997, and the products from his first production run sold out in less than a week. The revenues more than covered all of his operating costs, and provided him with some spending money and ready cash to continue operations.

Fortunately, John's attorney had patented John's designs, and only two weeks after his first sales, John got an offer from a parts manufacturer to purchase one of his patents for $2.3 million. John sold the patent, and immediately expanded his productive capability for his current products, and purchased some 'way cool' computer equipment and software to continue his design work at an even faster pace.

By the end of 2003, John had taken his shoestring business from infancy to maturity, a company with assets valued at $19.1 million. He was very fortunate to have hired business associates who seemed to be a great team, and had worked diligently to make the firm a success. John had started to reward the key members of his management team with shares of the firm's stock. In January 2004, John was approached by three analysts from an investment bank to take the firm public via an initial public offering of the firm's stock.

CURRENT CONDITION AND PERFORMANCE

Pearson Corporation produced a kind of following since its inception, and the news that John was considering offering stock to the public drew a high degree of attention. The story broke in the Charlotte newspaper, and John was getting inundated with phone calls asking for information about the company.

George Zans, one of the investment bankers, encouraged John to take advantage of the hype to promote his products and to hint about a possible date for the IPO. George told John that he needed some information from the company, including profit and loss statements, the current balance sheet, and other information specifically addressing how fast the firm was growing and what the prospects were for the coming year. The investment bank could provide a market analysis, and then an offering price had to be determined. George offered John a choice of distribution methods, a 'best efforts' or an 'underwritten' issue.

The company's summary information, market information, and details of the proposed distributions appear in Exhibits 1, 2, and 3.

Exhibit 1. Income Statement. Year Ended December 31, 2003.

Sales	$40,118,000
Variable Operating Costs	$16,542,000
Fixed Operating Costs	$19,898,000
Operating Profit	$3,678,000
Interest Expense	$634,608
Taxable Income	$3,043,392
Tax Expense	$958,668
NET INCOME	$2,084,724

Exhibit 2. Balance Sheet. December 31, 2003.

Current Assets:	
Cash	$789,000
Receivables	$3,901,000
Inventory	$3,002,000
Other	$1,209,000
Total Current Assets	$8,901,000
Net Fixed Assets	$10,203,000
TOTAL ASSETS	$19,104,000
Liabilities:	
Payables	$2,109,000
Short Term Notes	$1,932,000
Accrued Expenses	$1,200,000
Total Current Liabilities	$5,241,000
Long Term Debt	$4,895,000
Total Liabilities	$10,136,000
Common Stock	$6,000,000
Retained Earnings	$2,968,000
Total Equity	$8,968,000
TOTAL LIAB. + EQUITY	$19,104,000

Exhibit 3. Financial Data.

Dividends per Share, Past 7 years
(600,000 shares at $10 per share)

1997	$0.00
1998	$0.00
1999	$0.62
2000	$0.68
2001	$1.25
2002	$1.29
2003	$0.66

Sales Growth Rate (5 year)	16%
Earnings Growth Rate (5 year)	9.8%
Treasury Bond Rate	3.9%
Return on a Broad Market Index	10.74%
Beta (adjusted pure play)	1.58

REQUIRED

1. Based on information provided in the case, determine a value for the new shares for the IPO.

2. List advantages and disadvantages (for Pearson Corporation) concerning both the best efforts and the underwritten deals. Should John go with a best efforts or underwritten deal? Provide commentary on why you selected the method you did for Pearson.

3. Was the timing good for an IPO? What market characteristics should be taken into consideration for an IPO?

SECTION 3

BOND AND STOCK VALUATION

Case 6

SIMPLIFIED NETWORKING, INCORPORATED

KEEPING IT SIMPLE

Simplified Networking, Incorporated (SNI) had been founded in 1992 by Kenneth Gary. Before starting the company Gary had been an industrial engineer with a large international chemical firm. With nearly twenty years of 'working for the other guy,' Ken started his own company with hopes of eventually taking the firm public.

During the period of the 1990's the mid-western United States saw marked growth and renewed prosperity, after the "Rust Belt" era which had ended just a few years before. Economists documented economic growth in the region during this period of between four and six percent per year. Urban and industrial areas within the region saw even higher growth rates. As businesses expanded, there was a tremendous demand for integrated networks of desktop computers, and the development of new software and faster hardware made networks feasible for even the smallest companies. Ken had become familiar with the design of both local- and wide-area networks at his former job, and the intervening years had proved him right in following his instincts when creating Simplified Networking.

He created SNI in early 1992 with six friends and former subordinates. His role was "network engineer," which meant that he held certifications with the major networking software companies and was licensed to sell and install the network operating system software of each. In addition to being the president and CEO, Ken did the majority of the network design at the firm. He began with one other network engineer and three technicians, and kept the office staff down to a single person. As the business had expanded, the staff had grown in proportion.

Kenneth Gary's many years of business experience had been part of what attracted customers to his shop. In addition, he cultivated business relationships by being involved in several civic groups in his suburban town. He had always been a civic-minded fellow, and it was just natural for him to seek other successful leaders to work with. Folks came to Ken to talk about how they should run their businesses; after all, he had seen just about every type of business situation at one time or another. In the process of helping people through their crises, he gained the confidence and respect of the community. Through his involvement in charity and other groups, when he had the time, he quickly made a name for himself as someone who could be trusted. It was just natural, then, that folks seeking to learn about information technology and the benefits of networked computing would seek Ken out.

THE ART OF THE DEAL

Ken discounted his own selling ability when asked about it, but his colleagues would tell all who listened about his mastery of the "art of the deal." Ken Gary could break down a business problem as an expert would, and his ability to close a sale showed up quickly in SNI's revenue numbers. He easily combined networking technology with his business acumen, and SNI stayed busy. Ken constantly worked to recruit and train new engineers and technicians to provide the same expertise, and SNI had a generous continuing education program for employees. Many of the folks who had joined SNI since its early years had earned MBAs in addition to their technical certifications and degrees.

The computer networking industry throughout could be characterized as "fragmented" at the level of the firms which were responsible for the installation of the hardware and software. At that level, the business consisted of small companies known as "value-added resellers," whose characteristics varied a great deal from firm to firm. Each reseller configured desktop computers and installed one of several networking systems, depending upon the needs of the customer. In a study of the impact and scope of technology in U.S. businesses, a national research organization found that:

"The technology bubble of the late 1990s did not seem to impact the demand for distributed computing and networking services. Over the last five years (1998-2002) revenue growth has been strong, and the average cost of goods sold as a percent of sales has decreased somewhat. Net profit growth has been irregular due to the unpredictable behavior of selling and general administrative expenses, which increased sharply for some firms and declined slightly or stayed the same for others. Net income after-tax as a percent of sales has been in the range of 1.0% to 4.5%."

By 2003, SNI had become a recognized leader in its home state and had begun to expand regionally. Ken Gary finally started to see an opportunity to remove himself from the daily operations of the firm (retaining his role as "strategy guru") and perhaps even take the firm public with an issue of stock. He wanted to be able to spend more time with his family and charitable projects. Ken struggled with understanding how to take some cash out of the firm to provide a return for him and his senior employees while simultaneously retaining enough funds in the firm to keep it expanding and liquid. He quickly discovered that giving advice to others was much easier than formulating a master plan for something so important to his own welfare, and he knew that seeking outside opinions and assistance was the only responsible course of action.

TO IPO OR NOT TO IPO

Ken sought out a prominent local investment banker, Steve Jennings, with the intent of designing a public offering of the company's stock. When promoting the IPO, Jennings wanted to stress Ken's reputation in the business community and the reputation of SNI as a good employer and honest contractor. He also suggested that Ken should at least consider the prospect of issuing bonds as well as shares.

Jennings asked for some of SNI's operating information, and put together several exhibits in order to summarize the firm's success (Exhibits 1 and 2). In addition, he gathered information on the industry which he felt would be relevant to the financing decision (Exhibit 3). Jennings also summarized some capital market information which would be useful in figuring out the value of a bond issued by SNI.

Exhibit 1. Simplified Networking, Inc. Balance Sheet, December 31, 2003.

Current Assets	$1,200
Fixed Assets	$9,200
Total Assets	$10,400
Current Liabilities	$1,100
Mortgage Loans	$920
Common Stock ($1 par value)	$1,100
Retained Earnings	$7,280
Total Liabilities and Equity	$10,400

Exhibit 2. Revenue and Income Information (rounded).

Year	Revenue	Net Income (after taxes)
1993	$7,224,000	$236,000
1994	$7,624,000	$266,000
1995	$7,840,000	$274,000
1996	$7,960,000	$286,000
1997	$8,200,000	$310,000
1998	$8,648,000	$328,000
1999	$10,376,000	$394,000
2000	$12,002,000	$456,000
2001	$14,020,000	$546,000
2002	$15,000,000	$600,000
2003	$15,600,000	$624,000

Exhibit 3. Comparison Information.

Simplified Networking Incorporated
Composite Data (2003)
Networking Value-Added Resellers
Midwestern U.S. Five-Year Averages

Total debt as a percentage of total assets	20% - 32%
Compound growth in sales	9%
Compound growth in net income	8%
Dividend payout range	15% - 30%
Return on equity	15%
Average earnings per share	$3.00

Jennings' initial notes for Ken Gary included the following: "Capital market information as of year-end 2003 indicated that 10-year U.S. government bonds yielded 5.01%; the historical (past 10 years) yield on a broad market index of common stocks was 14%. The $1,000 face value bonds in the industry have an average coupon rate of 8 percent and have, on average, 10 years before maturity. I believe that new bonds issued at par in today's market (year-end 2003) would yield 6 percent. Finally, industry data for publicly-traded networking firms indicated that such firms' earnings were 20% more volatile than a benchmark market portfolio such as the Standard & Poors 500."

Jennings would not only have to satisfy, eventually, external investors, but his analysis would have to reassure Ken Gary that he was making the right decision by planning for the future of Simplified Networking.

In the upcoming months it would become apparent whether Ken Gary's devotion to his customers, neighbors and employees had been enough to allow SNI to move ahead to the next stage of its evolution: becoming a public company. Just as had happened when leaving his former employer many years before, the decision weighed heavily on Ken Gary and caused many sleepless nights. With the necessary planning, though, he was confident that SNI would be a better, more flexible company afterward.

REQUIRED:

1. Evaluate the current market conditions and discuss some advantages and disadvantages of SNI going public. Is Gary making the right decision? Why or why not?

2. Comment on the interrelationship between taking the firm public and its reputation, managerial depth and skill, and operating history.

3. Discuss the company's core business and its potential over the next 3-5 years. What factors will likely contribute most significantly to the company' success or failure?

4. Is it reasonable for founders such as Ken Gary to seek to 'liquidate' part of SNI's value after building the company over several years? Discuss this in terms of his personal goals and the future of the company.

5. What is the role of the investment banker in this decision, and in general? Is Ken Gary at a likely disadvantage because of his own lack of objectivity? Please explain.

6. What is the likely initial public offering (IPO) price for the company's stock? (For the stock price calculation, assume that the relevant industry data will also apply to SNI.) Assume that an investor's required return on a stock of this type can be derived from the capital market data given and the information in Exhibit 3.

7. For practice, determine what the price should be for the comparable industry bonds mentioned. Your analysis should highlight the interrelationship among the bond's face value, coupon rate, current yield and price. Does the comparable bond's price give any useful information regarding the proposed stock IPO? Does the change in interest rates (for the industry) suggest that a debt issue might be preferable to a stock issue?

8. What additional information would be useful in this decision to go public? Name some likely sources for such information. Please be specific, and explain your answer.

Case 7

FINSIM MODELING, INCORPORATED

Eric Williams had to cut the weekly meeting short. "That's done. Same time next week." he told them. The technical gurus of the company had started to take over the conversation again, waxing eloquent about the latest and greatest algorithm they had found to include in the firm's namesake software package. Williams' cousin Brian Edwards was the most vocal of the tech types, and he encouraged spontaneous discussions of this kind, even when there was a full list of more important things to discuss. "More important to the business, but not more important to most of these folks" thought Williams. He had always looked upon this job as much the same as being the ringmaster at a three-ring circus.

Williams had hoped to discuss another topic today, but he conceded defeat. The firm's rapid growth and optimistic sales estimates had brought out another, older concern: when would the firm go public with its stock? Williams had spent a great deal of time with this, and he knew that the question lingered in the minds of everyone at the meeting. They were all shareholders, in any case. As the week progressed, Williams hoped to get enough information together to warrant bringing it up at next week's meeting.

FinSim represented a unique challenge for Eric Williams. His many years of experience in finance and management had not prepared him for managing computer programmers and academics. He thought the problem may have been the nature of academic work itself; most professors were used to working long hours and having lots of freedom to investigate almost any idea, profitable or not. Williams had managed to keep the firm focused and productive only with his cousin's help in managing the talent.

OUR SOFTWARE GOES TO ELEVEN

The company had a single product: the FinSim modeling package. FinSim had originated as a research project of Brian Edwards and several of his colleagues at a nearby university. After securing the rights to their efforts, this small group had left their careers and formed FinSim to try to capitalize on their ideas. The software was in its tenth release, and version eleven (V. 11) had been outstanding in beta form for several months. There were "power users" and academics from many different fields willing to help the company test the newest version before it was made available to the public. The enthusiasm that the beta testers showed for the new capabilities of the software was promising (financially) and fulfilling (intellectually) for the folks involved. The newest FinSim would probably be a hit with those already using the software, and would likely help the firm gain market share and find new users.

FinSim software allowed users to create, test and use neural network analysis models. Over time, more and more of the company's clients had begun using neural networks for business or financial applications, but the FinSim software itself, as originally conceived, proved versatile enough for almost any application users could think up. FinSim led the industry, by virtue of its age, expertise and reliability, and had already experienced tremendous growth at the expense of its competitors with earlier versions of the software. In addition, FinSim had reached a major milestone with V. 11: for the first time, the company would be able to update its software without creating major revisions every year or so. In addition, they would be able to produce software for several different platforms (Microsoft, Apple, Unix, etc.) simultaneously. This was due to advances in programming software, and FinSim had restructured itself in the last few years to be able to make this an important part of the latest release and the support structure behind it. It was an innovative approach, but the tech folks at FinSim had made it look easy.

Williams and some of his tech managers had compiled their best estimates of how the new release would impact the sales and earnings of the company (Exhibit 1). They had carefully considered the impact of the new programming system as well. After its release, V. 11 was likely to grow very rapidly over a four year period, with a return to industry-level growth values after that as the software started to mature and competitors regained some of their edge. None of the folks involved were particularly worried about FinSim's market share; after four years of extraordinary growth, and with the advancements in the new software design and content, it would extremely hard for FinSim to be knocked from the top of the hill. Some of the best minds in the software business had been polled on this, informally, and felt that FinSim was in a particularly unusual and advantageous position.

NEURAL NETWORKS

When he had decided to help his cousin run the company, Eric Williams made it very plain from the start that most of the technical details were beyond his comprehension. He had told his cousin "I just want to do the business stuff. You guys work out the rest." Over time, though, he had found neural networks, and the business of his customers, to be easy to understand and interesting.

Exhibit 1. FinSim Modeling Inc. Selected Company Data (as of 4th Quarter 2003).

Forecasted sales growth: compound annual rate	31.4%
Estimated net income growth: compound annual annual rate (estimated duration: 4 years)	24.7%
Projected sustainable net income growth, beyond 4 years	12.3%
Projected dividend payout during the rapid growth period growth period (over the next 4 years)	18.8%
Projected dividend payout after high growth period	32.7%
Investors' required return on new FinSim stock	15.6%

Neural networks simulated the action of simple nerve cells, or neurons, by allowing for interconnections and memory within a network of analysis steps. Unlike most tools used for economic forecasting, for instance, neural networks allowed researchers to "train" the model with new data as it arrived. In addition, because neural networks processed data in a parallel fashion, there was a potential reduction in processing time to be gained in many applications. Both of these advantages, and the ability to use neural networks to find interesting patterns in otherwise random data, had brought the technique to the notice of many economists and business researchers around the world. In business, neural nets had been used to forecast exchange rates, measure bankruptcy risk, coordinate direct mail advertising, and predict market crashes, among other applications. They had also been used to predict weather and the migration patterns of whales. As the uses of neural computing became more evident over time, FinSim had managed to keep its place at the top of the industry.

To maintain its leadership, the company had always recruited the brightest, and often the most expensive, researchers in the world. It was known for having the best development folks in the business. It also had an excellent reputation for customer support. In addition, FinSim consultants worked daily with many of the largest firms in the country, providing modeling services and technical support that none of the competitors had been able to duplicate. Version 11 was designed to appeal to a much wider base of users, and most of the folks at FinSim were pleased with their accomplishment.

THE DECISION AT HAND

As the company began to roll out V.11, the managers and other senior staff struggled with the decision of whether or not to go public with the firm's shares. In the early years it had been acceptable to keep the firm closely-held; after all, even the most tech-savvy venture capitalists had been less than eager to back a fledging firm with a highly technical product. It was almost ten years later, and with plenty of name recognition and high profile customers FinSim was a viable prospect for external equity financing. Their additions to the software were gaining a great deal of press coverage, and it suddenly appeared to be an opportune time for resolving what Williams referred to as "the financing question."

In addition, many of the owners had started to ask Williams about whether they should consider different types of investments in order to diversify and limit their risks. In order for most of them to be able to diversify they would first need to be able to sell part of their interest in FinSim. As a trained financier, Williams understood the value of diversification at both the personal and corporate levels, and he was determined to help his people straighten things out.

In close consultation with one of the firm's customers, a large multinational investment bank, Williams had assembled several years' worth of financial statements (Exhibits 2 and 3) as well as some market information that would be useful when making the decision to go public (Exhibit 4). The folks at the investment bank had also spent a great deal of time with the reasoning and marketing information behind Exhibit 1, making sure that these numbers were reasonable and representative. In their opinion, the future of FinSim would rest on the success of its next software release.

Exhibit 2. FinSim Modeling, Inc. Balance Sheets (December 31).

	1999	2000	2001	2002	2003
Current assets:					
Cash	$485,625	$495,338	$505,244	$515,349	$525,656
Accounts receivable	$175,750	$179,265	$182,850	$186,507	$190,237
Inventory	$18,500	$18,870	$19,247	$19,632	$20,025
Prepaid expenses	$8,325	$8,492	$8,661	$8,835	$9,011
Total current assets	$688,200	$701,964	$716,003	$730,323	$744,930
Fixed assets:					
Net property	$1,748,250	$1,765,733	$1,783,390	$1,801,224	$1,819,236
Office equipment, net	$5,536,125	$5,702,209	$5,873,275	$6,049,473	$6,230,957
Total assets	$7,972,575	$8,169,905	$8,372,668	$8,581,020	$8,795,123
Liabilities:					
Notes payable	$2,764,806	$2,901,009	$3,033,142	$3,159,919	$3,279,845
Accounts payable	$185,000	$194,250	$203,963	$214,161	$224,869
Total liabilities	$2,949,806	$3,095,259	$3,237,105	$3,374,080	$3,504,714
Shareholder equity:					
Common stock (at par)	$344,655	$344,655	$344,655	$344,655	$344,655
Paid-in-capital	$4,625,000	$4,625,000	$4,625,000	$4,625,000	$4,625,000
Retained earnings	$53,114	$104,991	$165,909	$237,285	$320,754
Total liabilities and equity	$7,972,575	$8,169,905	$8,372,668	$8,581,020	$8,795,123

Exhibit 3. FinSim Modeling, Inc. Income Statements (ended December 31).

	1999	2000	2001	2002	2003
Sales revenue	$2,035,000	$2,340,250	$2,691,288	$3,094,981	$3,559,228
Software consulting	$277,500	$319,125	$366,994	$422,043	$485,349
Net sales	$2,312,500	$2,659,375	$3,058,281	$3,517,023	$4,044,577
Costs and expenses:					
Salaries	$925,000	$952,750	$981,333	$1,010,772	$1,041,096
Marketing	$323,750	$336,700	$350,168	$364,175	$378,742
General and administrative expense	$254,375	$256,919	$259,488	$262,083	$264,704
Research and development	$346,875	$388,500	$435,120	$487,334	$545,815
Total cost and expenses	$1,850,000	$1,934,869	$2,026,108	$2,124,364	$2,230,356
Operating income:	$462,500	$724,506	$1,032,173	$1,392,659	$1,814,221
Interest expense	$194,250	$194,250	$194,250	$194,250	$194,250
Earnings before taxes	$268,250	$530,256	$837,923	$1,198,409	$1,619,971
Taxes	$91,205	$180,287	$284,894	$407,459	$550,790
Net income	$177,045	$349,969	$553,029	$790,950	$1,069,181
Dividends paid	$123,932	$244,978	$387,120	$553,665	$748,427
Retained earnings	$53,114	$104,991	$165,909	$237,285	$320,754

Exhibit 4. Industry/Market Characteristics (17 publicly traded firms represented).

Average stock price, software peer firms	$100
Range of prices	$70 - $150
Median price/earnings ratio	60x
Average earnings per share (EPS)	$4.00
Stock return volatility compared to market average (beta)	1.2
Average payout ratio	30%
Average EPS growth	10%
Average yield on 5-year Treasury bonds	5%
Historical market risk premium	8.50%
Beta for the Dow Jones Industrial Average	1

REQUIRED

1. Describe the company's business and its potential over the next 3-5 years.

2. What is the compound rate of net sales increase over the years shown?

3. Discuss the appropriateness of taking the firm public, given the characteristics of the industry and the firm's operating environment. What are some of the factors that enter into the decision to go public at any firm?

4. Discuss the ownership structure of the company and how this might influence the decision to offer public shares.

5. What is a likely initial public offering (IPO) stock price for the company given the case data and the assumed initial earnings per share of $4? Be sure to consider both expected stages of future sales and income growth.

6. Comment on the past and projected sales growth. What influence does that growth have on the firm's decision to go public?

7. What additional data would be useful to the company's management and the investment bankers as they prepare for the IPO? Please be specific and explain your reasoning.

8. As a 'benchmark', does the industry data seem adequate for the decision facing the company? Why and/or why not?

Case 8

FRED ALBERTS, ROOKIE

FRED'S ACCOUNT

Fred pressed the 'return' key, carrying out the trades he had figured would give him a good return. He had opened the online stock trading account in order to learn about the process of trading and to take advantage of his academic knowledge of how the markets determine stock values. He had taken several finance classes in his undergraduate degree, and had enjoyed learning the way investors decide how much to bid on stocks. Fred figured he could take advantage of this knowledge in creating more wealth than he could if he just invested in an investment fund.

THE BROKER'S ADVICE

When he opened the trading account, Fred had signed up for telephone access to a broker. The account allowed him a certain number of calls and a certain amount of time in consultation with the broker each month. Now, Fred had quite a sum of free cash in the account, money he had transferred from an investment fund that he was not very happy with. The amount he had to invest was about $68,000. He decided to take advantage of the advisement service, and made his first telephone call.

"Welcome to Bettertrade services, Mr. Alberts. My name is Brad Cendron. How can I assist you today?", the voice asked.

"Yes; I would like to get your advice on how to invest a sum of money. My objective is to invest this amount in stocks that appear to be undervalued by the market. Can you recommend about ten stocks that would fit that description?", Fred asked.

"Oh, yes, I'd be happy to. We have listed our top bargains on the "top stock picks" list on the website. Are you online now?", Brad asked.

"Yes, I am," Fred replied. "Oh, I see it here. They are in order, according to your idea of how much of a bargain they are, right?"

"That's correct, Mr. Albert. We believe that these 20 stocks are going to have greater upside potential over time. I can help you make the transactions, if you'd like."

"Well, I'm going to do a little more research on my own first, but thank you for the link. I'll just carry out transactions via the website, since the transaction fees are lower that way," Fred said.

"OK, Mr. Albert," Brad replied. Let us know if you have other questions, or if we can assist you further."

Fred printed out the list of stocks, and set about the task of collecting information about them. He went to the "market data" link on the company's website to get some information. For each firm, he downloaded the history of dividend payments, and the beta. He also downloaded current treasury bond rates and the rate of return on a broad market index, which he would use as an indicator of the market return. Fred summarized the information and prepared to determine the value of the stocks according to the financial models he had studied in college.

Fred's collection of information and the current market prices of the stocks in the "top stock picks" list from his broker appear in Exhibits 1, 2, and 3.

Exhibit 1. Top 20 Stock Picks List.

Stock Rank	Price, 1/05/04
1	$14.89
2	$29.02
3	$18.83
4	$93.48
5	$67.29
6	$3.28
7	$9.00
8	$55.91
9	$98.47
10	$43.07
11	$37.55
12	$38.30
13	$76.33
14	$67.09
15	$193.05
16	$38.33
17	$71.11
18	$9.23
19	$19.35
20	$29.92

Exhibit 2. Dividend Histories and Beta.

Stock Rank	Total Dividend, 2003	5-Year Dividend Growth	Beta
1	$0.95	0.58%	0.74
2	$0.00	-100.00%	2.3
3	$0.00	0.00%	1.89
4	$1.25	8.50%	1.31
5	$0.78	1.25%	1.52
6	$0.06	-9.00%	1.04
7	$0.00	-100.00%	1.99
8	$0.00	0.00%	0.89
9	$6.22	0.98%	1.06
10	$1.00	-0.48%	1.76
11	$0.00	-100.00%	0.91
12	$0.25	2.10%	1.8
13	$0.98	-2.00%	0.82
14	$2.25	4.00%	1.12
15	$5.80	-8.00%	0.99
16	$1.02	13.00%	1.01
17	$6.00	5.00%	0.67
18	$0.00	0.00%	1.11
19	$1.00	9.00%	0.78
20	$0.00	-100.00%	1.2

*dividend growth is the compound growth rate between D_{t-5} and D_0

Exhibit 3. Other Financial Information.

Treasury Bond Rate (historical)	4.1%
Return on a Broad Market Index	12.1%

Exhibit 4. Formulas from Fred's Old Textbooks.

Constant Growth Valuation Model:

$$V_{CS} = \frac{D_1}{k_{equity} - g}$$

V_{CS} is the value of the share of common stock
D_1 is the expected dividend (the last paid dividend times 1+g)
k_{equity} is the required return (Fred would use the CAPM to determine this)
g is the growth rate of the dividend

Capital Asset Pricing Model Formula:

$$k_{equity} = k_{RF} + \beta(k_M - k_{RF})$$

k_{equity} is the required return on the common shares
k_{RF} is the rate of return on treasury bonds
k_M is the rate of return on a broad market index
β is a measure of systematic risk for the company (the 'beta')

REQUIRED

1. For each stock listed, calculate the required return as indicated by the Capital Asset Pricing Model (CAPM).

2. Calculate the value of each stock share using the constant growth formula.

3. Compare the values you calculated to each of the market prices for the top twenty stock picks. Are your calculations close approximations of the market prices? Why do you think there are differences?

4. What are the implications of your analysis to Fred's choice of stocks?

5. Think about your results in terms of claims of market efficiency. On average, over the long term, do you think that the models you used to calculate the stock values really works? Why or why not?

6. In light of your answer in number 5 above, how would you advise Fred?

SECTION 4

CAPITAL BUDGETING DECISIONS

CASE 9

PERFORMANCE BOATING PRODUCTS, INC.

INTRODUCTION

Performance Boating Products, Inc. (PBP) is a producer of attachments for boat hulls and motors that aid watercraft in reducing drag and maintaining 'plane'. The attachments can be manufactured as a part of new boats, or retrofitted to older boats and motors. PBP's customers are usually boaters wanting an extra degree of performance from their boats, and boat manufacturers offering PBP products as options.

THE BOARDROOM

Sam Cutlowe sat in the plush boardroom chair, trying to mentally sift through the unorganized flow of information from the firm's different functional managers. Ultimately, it would become his responsibility to make financially sound recommendations to Mr. Slater, the CFO of Performance Boating Products, Inc. regarding the three potential investments the firm was considering funding.

"Are you listening to me, Sam?" It was K.K. Morgan, the marketing division manager. "I have a complete breakdown of our sales projections by region, for each project. Hope you appreciate the time and effort of putting that together!" Morgan was a large, domineering person, and seemed perturbed about Sam's presence. Morgan also seemed to have difficulty realizing that sales projections were really a common thing to deal with for most marketing people. "Yes, I can appreciate the effort," Sam responded. "A good sales forecast sure is essential for good decisions to result. Thanks." Morgan puffed up as he heard the subtle praise. In Sam's experience, it was good to have the favor of the other managers.

Mr. Goodson, the company's CEO, responded "Well, isn't that sweet. Let's get on with it. Do you have the cost estimates?" He was directing the question at Wetsel, a quiet, reserved man who headed up the firm's accounting department.

"Yes, sir." Wetsel pulled a two inch thick document from his briefcase. "Here are all of the figures, organized by project." He slid the papers to Sam.

A moment passed, and an awkward silence was broken by the roar of Goodson: "Well, Sam. Get to it!" Goodson used the phrase "get to it!" to indicate his expectation of activity, whether the task was immediately addressed or not. Sam excused himself and quickly exited the room. He was just as happy to get out of the meeting and "get to it." He always seemed to be called on the carpet in the meetings, and as far as he could tell, he was the one person who had additional work to do whenever the meetings ended.

ASSEMBLING PROJECTIONS

The paperwork Sam acquired at the board meeting mainly consisted of sales projections from the firm's sales force and cost projections from accounting, broken down into the three projects under consideration. All three were asset expansion projects that would produce products for which there appeared to be demand from PBP customers.

Sam had been surprised at the prices PBP products were able to command in the market. The markup was a considerable markup for products that, though protected by copyright, seemed to be fairly simple to duplicate in purpose. The attachments for boat hulls and motors were basic metal and fiberglass structures. The attachments could be manufactured into new products, or retrofitted to older boats and motors. They had commanded excellent prices in the past. Thus far, the firm had been able to sell all that they produced, and the demand appeared to exceed PBP's capability to produce.

The first project was called "Melville." It involved the construction of a new warehouse in a strategic location. It would not only increase sales in the geographic area, it would also reduce distribution costs. The second project, "Broadside," was another production facility where the same aluminum fins would be manufactured. From the feedback from the regional sales reps, one problem PBP faced was that the products were not readily available. There was always a backlog of orders. The new facility was expected to alleviate the problem. The other project was called "the turbine project" because of the new type of apparatus that would be produced, and because a site had not yet been decided upon. Sam was told by Slater to "just estimate a site cost, and have some justification for your estimate." Sam developed an estimate based on the large number of similar site costs available from the manager of the industrial park where the facility would locate.

Sam summarized the marketing and accounting estimates of projected sales and costs for each project (Exhibit 1). Since the projects appeared to be of average risk for the firm, Sam didn't see any reason for risk adjustments. All three were expected to have nearly equal lives, and they were not mutually exclusive, so no adjustment appeared necessary concerning unequal lives. They were all fairly large projects for the firm, though. Sam therefore considered preciseness and accuracy of his analysis to be very important.

COST OF CAPITAL

PBP's cost of capital was well-documented, and it was a relatively small task for Sam to adjust the estimates for the expansion projects, taking into account expected changes in risk. Sam decided to use three methods for estimating the cost of equity: the Discounted Cash Flow (DCF) method, the Capital Asset Pricing Model (CAPM) method, and the Bond Yield + Risk Premium (BY+RP) method. He had learned all three during his MBA schooling, and figured he may as well cover all the bases just in case Mr. Goodson or one of the other managers was critical of one method or the other.

For each of the three methods, Sam decided that he would present cost graphs for the marginal cost of capital, which would be useful later for overlaying the internal rate of return. The graphs appear in Figures 1-3.

PROJECT RETURNS

For the three projects under consideration, Sam decided that he would calculate internal rates of return (IRR) for each project. The three projects were fairly normal (i.e. a large cost up front and then positive cashflows thereafter) so the mathematical problems with IRR calculation, he reasoned, shouldn't make a big difference. He also preferred IRR because everyone seemed to understand it, especially with respect to the firm's cost of capital. Since there were alternative methods of calculating cost of capital, it would also be easy to see the effect that each method had on the capital budget, if any.

All of the projects were independent of one another, and all three required either full investment or none - no partial investment in any of the three projects was possible.

THE TASK

All the preliminary work had been done. Sam decided that he would allot a block of time to concentrate on the task at hand - analyzing the wealth of information that had been gathered. This was in addition to his normal duties at the firm, so Sam decided to dedicate the weekend to the task. There would be fewer distractions, he could work at home, and he felt he could have the task completed by Monday.

Exhibit 1. Summary of Project Characteristics.

	Melville Project	Broadside Project	Turbine Project
Initial Cost (net investment)	$10.1 million	$9.2 million	$16.9 million
Incremental Annual Sales	$4,398,000	$4,126,000	$7,620,000
Incremental Annual Cash Oper. Costs	$1,980,000	$1,830,000	$3,855,000
Estimated Project Life	30 years	30 years	28 years
MACRS Category	15 year	15 year	15 year

Exhibit 2. MACRS 15-Year Depreciation Schedule.

year	MACRS %	year	MACRS %	year	MACRS %
1	5	6	6.23	11	5.91
2	9.5	7	5.9	12	5.9
3	8.55	8	5.9	13	5.91
4	7.7	9	5.91	14	5.9
5	6.93	10	5.9	15	5.91
				16	2.95

Figure 1. Marginal Cost of Capital Schedule using Discounted Cash Flow.

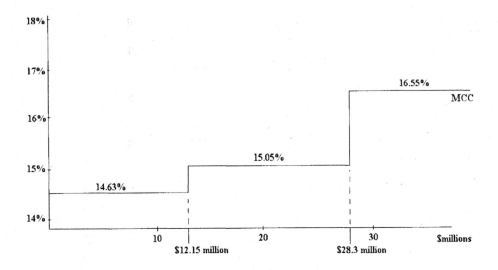

Figure 2. Marginal Cost of Capital Using CAPM for Cost of Equity.

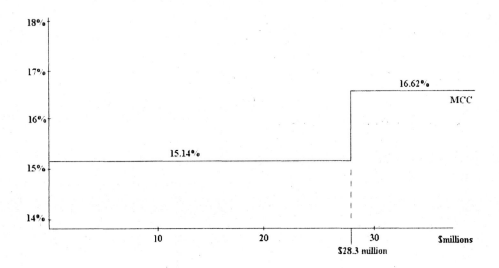

Figure 3. Marginal Cost of Capital Using BY+RP approach for Cost of Equity.

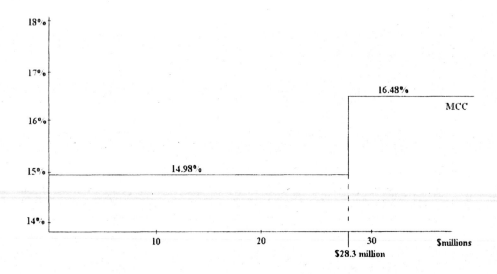

REQUIRED:

1. Using a spreadsheet program such as Excel, calculate incremental net cashflows for each year for the three projects (hint - use a different worksheet for each project).

2. Using your cashflow estimates from #1, use the spreadsheet to determine the internal rate of return (IRR) for each project using the trial-and-error method.

3. Plot the investment opportunity schedule on each of Sam's MCC graphs. Evaluate each project. For the marginal project, show the calculations from your evaluation.

4. Should the marginal project be accepted or not? Do the three cost of capital methods agree as to the accept/reject decision?

5. Discuss the relative strengths/weaknesses of the DCF, CAPM, and BY+RP methods for determining cost of capital.

Case 10

BENTLEY CUSTOM CERAMICS

The last pieces of a twenty-foot-long decorative brick wall were just coming out of the firing kiln. Julian Bentley jumped as the telephone rang, dropping the last brick for the wall, but fortunately, it did not break. Julian answered the phone. It was Mr. Reynolds, a loan officer from the bank.

"Your loan's been approved," Reynolds said. "Just come sign the papers and you can order your new kiln."

Reynolds had really gone to bat for Julian at the bank to get his loan approved. He had been a satisfied customer from way back. Four years ago, when Reynolds bought his "dream house" in Williamsburg, he had been exceptionally impressed by an interior wall of relief sculpture done in brick. He had called the contractor for the house and found out about Julian, who had produced the brick. He contracted Julian to do another relief sculpture and a mosaic tile work and was favorably impressed by both.

In fact, it was Reynold's suggestion that Julian consider expanding the business. Initially, Julian had considered himself to be a "starving artist," making enough money to survive while doing what he loved to do: work with ceramic arts. He had not counted on a continuing stream of contracts from Williamsburg's prestige-seeking residents. Initially, he had worked on a few small projects for extra money while running a craft shop on Route 60 just south of Williamsburg. He sold ceramic items custom made by him, and products made by other local artists.

A milestone event happened five years ago, however. A shop patron who Julian really didn't like had seen some of the small projects Julian had done for an executive for Castle Green Country Club, and "just had to have" an original brick work in *her* house, as well. Julian, not wanting anything to do with that customer, quoted a ridiculously high price for the requested work. To Julian's surprise, she had immediately written a check for half of his price, and said she would pay the rest upon completion of the job. Word of mouth soon found Julian enjoying plenty of brick and mosaic jobs at premium prices. He had a six-month backlog of work, and was running his ceramic kiln all day, every day, except for increasing downtime when the kiln needed maintenance and repair.

The need for new productive equipment and employees to handle the non-artistic aspects of the business became increasingly apparent. Julian felt that he could meet his current demand, and even expand his business by investing in better production equipment. He had also considered making molds for certain designs that had special appeal, and producing limited runs of the design. It would not be custom artwork, but Julian felt there may be demand for limited run brick art, as well.

"We have also arranged for a working capital loan and a line of credit for you," Reynolds said. "The loans will be secured by the equipment, and by your property in Lee Hall." Lee Hall was a small community about ten miles from Williamsburg, where Julian owned a house and seven acres of land, a family property he had inherited free of mortgages.

"Thank you, Mr. Reynolds. I'll be in touch," replied Julian.

EQUIPMENT

One of the decisions Julian had wrestled with was the choice between an electric and a gas-fired kiln. Julian had used an electric kiln for years, and had been pleased with their ease of firing thin flat ceramic objects, such as tile or thin brick fascia, or tall pieces requiring even heating. Julian liked the idea that no flammable gas was used, and that all he had to do was turn the kiln on to start the process. The greatest problem with his electric kiln was that it was very expensive to run. Using electricity to provide heat was not very cost effective, he thought, and he was concerned that a high capacity electric kiln would be prohibitively costly to run. The kiln had also been fairly costly to maintain and repair.

Gas fired kilns had nice features that offset the electric kilns' problems. For one thing, the heat was much more uniform within the kiln, creating more consistency of the product. Temperature control was easier, and quickly adjusted. Certain glazing colors were possible with fire that were not possible with electric heating. Gas kilns typically were available in a wider variety of sizes, and large production kilns could yield large quantities of product quickly. One of the best features of gas was that it was cheap to operate. One of Julian's fellow artists in Richmond said that he ran his 92 cubic foot kiln for only $7.10 per burn, on average. The kiln was about a 4.5 foot cube, with shelves inside for layering items.

What Julian was considering was a 'bank' of three units, each having a 78 cubic foot capacity. Julian reasoned that small production runs could be handled by one or two kilns, but he could also run all three for large jobs. The gas kilns were $27,000 each, a total investment of $81,000 plus around $4,800 for installation and expert testing. Julian figured that if he went to gas firing, he certainly wanted them to be as safe as possible.

The same volume capacity could be accomplished with twelve electric units, costing $3750 each. The installation would only be $800 for an industrial electric service. Julian was not looking forward to having to set up all twelve units for large jobs. He also had concerns that the quality (uniformity) of the product would suffer, not only because of the inconsistencies *within* the single units, but also because of differences *between* the units.

The only information Julian had to assist in the decisions was an operational cost summary provided by Production Testing Service, Inc., which had estimated energy usage under normal running conditions. Fortunately, the information was available for both of the types of kilns he was considering. He felt certain that the numbers had meaning. His limited understanding of analytical matters, however, handicapped him in terms of understanding their significance.

Although his financing package had been approved by the bank, he wondered whether Reynold's insistence about his approval was justified by the feasibility of the planned expansion. He also wondered about which kiln alternative was better in the long run. Julian freely admitted that he was not a very effective businessman, and had no idea about how to determine if the investment would produce a satisfactory financial result for him. He felt very fortunate to have developed a reputation that allowed him to have such a substantial gap between the price he charged for his work and the direct cost of the raw materials and operating costs. Julian was also a bit uneasy about borrowing, especially if he had to pledge the family home for collateral.

THE QUESTION

Julian had been advised by Mr. Reynolds about the importance of projected sales and expense information when applying for a business loan. Julian had provided Reynolds with some cost projections. Julian felt the projections were realistic; he had been fairly conservative, understating his expected sales amounts and overstating expenses slightly (see Exhibit 4). He was unsure about the extra utilities expenses associated with either type of kiln, but had provided Reynolds the other figures. That was part of the reason Julian was puzzled by the sudden loan approval. Had Reynolds done some kind of analysis of Julian's figures? Or had he just pushed the loan application through?

Exhibit 1. Production Testing Service, Inc. Data

Model 10/92 Gas Fired Kiln

Fuel Type	Capacity	Fuel/Avg Use	Unit Cost
propane	78 cu.ft	15.6 lb/burn	$0.498/lb.

General Lee 20 Electric Kiln

Fuel Type	Capacity	Fuel/Avg Use	Unit Cost
electric 220/3	18.9 cu.ft	5.986 kwh/burn	$1.46/kwh**

* lb. represents a standard measure of a unit of liquid propane, a pound.
** kwh represents a standard measure of a unit of electric power, kilowatt hour.

Exhibit 2. Income Statements.

Bentley Custom Ceramics
Income Statements

	1997	1998	1999
Revenues:			
Brick Revenues	$103,089.00	$121,010.00	$154,322.00
Cost of Goods Sold			
Beginning Inventory	$19,892.00	$30,022.00	$39,994.00
	$50,808.00	$58,686.00	$74,547.00
Purchases			
Less: End. Inventory	$30,022.00	$39,994.00	$60,109.00
Cost of Goods Sold	$40,678.00	$48,714.00	$54,432.00
Gross Margin	$62,411.00	$72,296.00	$99,890.00
Operating Expenses:			
Advertising Expense	$351.00	$509.00	$541.00
Car & Truck Expense	$1,523.00	$2,019.00	$2,295.00
Depreciation Expense	$2,000.00	$6,058.00	$9,676.00
Insurance Expense	$1,486.00	$2,094.00	$2,392.00
Interest Expense	$0.00	$0.00	$0.00
Prof. Fees Expense	$1,000.00	$1,100.00	$1,100.00
Office Expense	$952.00	$1,050.00	$1,155.00
Rent Expense	$9,000.00	$9,000.00	$9,000.00
Repairs Expense	$1,559.00	$2,053.00	$3,303.00
Supplies Expense	$4,754.00	$6,509.00	$6,925.00
Tax Expense	$1,865.00	$2,817.00	$2,900.00
Utilities Expense	$5,007.00	$6,020.00	$7,002.00
Wage Expense	$5,070.00	$10,101.00	$10,049.00
Other Expense	$1,439.00	$1,507.00	$1,512.00
Total Expense	$36,006.00	$50,837.00	$57,850.00
Net Income	$26,405.00	$21,459.00	$42,040.00

Exhibit 3. Balance Sheets

Bentley Custom Ceramics
Balance Sheets

	1997	1998	1999
Assets			
Cash	$2,502.00	$3,072.00	$3,542.00
Accounts Receivable	$9,989.00	$19,989.00	$39,452.00
Inventory	$30,022.00	$39,994.00	$60,109.00
Prop. Plant & Equip.	$10,104.00	$30,058.00	$48,990.00
Less:Acc. Depreciation	$2,000.00	$8,058.00	$17,734.00
Net Prop. Plant & Equip.	$8,104.00	$22,000.00	$31,256.00
Total Assets	$40,628.00	$65,066.00	$94,907.00

Liabilities			
Accounts Payable	$20,128.00	$30,124.00	$59,141.00
Notes Payable	$0.00	$0.00	$0.00
Total Liabilities	$20,128.00	$30,124.00	$59,141.00
Owner's Equity			
Bentley Capital	$20,500.00	$34,942.00	$35,766.00
Total Liab. and Equity	$40,628.00	$65,066.00	$94,907.00

Exhibit 4. Sales and Cost Projections.

* Productivity and capacity assumed to be approximately the same for either project (12 electric units versus 3 propane gas units)
* Project's useful life: 15 years
* 7.5 year asset depreciation range (ADR) midpoint

*Sales Projection: Additional $176,000 per year ($8,000 per extra job on average)
*Total annual number of extra capacity firings per year (over and above his current production): 22

*Incremental Cash Operating Expenses projections:
> Cost of goods sold: $70,400 more per year
> No additional car/truck expense, professional fees, or office expenses
> $500 more in advertising per year
> $2200 more insurance per year
> $600 more repair expense per year
> Increase in interest expense because of the 9% loan (Julian was unable to estimate this cost)
> No change in rent- still seven years left on ten year lease Higher utilities (electric OR gas) which had to be estimated based on PTS data
> Higher depreciation expense, because of the new equipment. Julian would get his accountant to estimate this using the MACRS standard.
> Supplies expense- higher by $800 per year
> Wages expense- higher by $5,000 per year

REQUIRED

Assume you have been asked to analyze the decisions faced by Julian Bentley. Among the tasks involved are:

1. Calculate net operating cashflows for both projects, using appropriate depreciation schedules.

2. What are the implications of mutually exclusive projects; would you characterize the gas and electric kilns as mutually exclusive; why or why not?

3. What is the appropriate cost of capital to use for discounting expected future cashflows?

4. Evaluate both alternatives using appropriate capital budgeting decision criteria.

Case 11

LEHMAN CONTAINER CORPORATION

A LOUD MEETING

Shawn Weatherbee, chief executive officer for Lehman Container Corporation, breathed a sigh of frustration. A rather heated meeting had just occurred with Stan Leftwich, the marketing manager for the firm, Bob Trawick, operations manager, and Vice President Lee Wallen, Shawn's executive assistant. All three of them seemed dead set on their own ideas about the direction the firm should take concerning the company's new investment opportunities.

Shawn pressed the intercom switch. "Laura, will you come get this tape?" His secretary entered the room and took the audio tape from the meeting.

"If you can make sense out of it, I'd appreciate a summary of each of their positions. Try to narrow it down to what each of them wants to do. Oh - you can skip the profanity. Hopefully there will be a few words left after you do that," Shawn said.

"I'll do my best," Laura replied.

Shawn picked up the phone and pressed an extension. "Hello, Howard. I need you to do some overtime for me. Have you done an analysis of financial feasibility - like for investment projects?....Well, I'll tell you what I need. I want to have some numbers run on the five projects we are considering for the coming year. One is just a regular project - either we do it or we don't, depending on whether the benefits exceed the cost. Two of the others are competing projects; we do one or the other, subject, of course, to either one covering costs. The other two are also competing projects for the new computing facility. We'll go with either Sun or IBM, so we need to get the numbers on each one." Shawn paused as he listened to the response. "That's great," Shawn said. "I knew I could count on you. After you get this for me, you can take some time off, OK? Later." Shawn had been talking to Howard Ledbetter, an accountant who had been with the firm for two years. He and Shawn had been college buddies and had graduated together eight years ago. Howard had always seemed to understand most aspects of business, able to bring diverse information together for a cohesive 'big picture.'

Now, Shawn hoped Howard would provide him with some rational thought and numerical justification for some of the decisions that had to be made concerning the capital budget.

HOWARD LEDBETTER'S TASK

As Howard hung up the phone, a slight smile came across his face. He could just imagine the dynamics of the big meeting that had been held earlier. The company's officers were, to put it mildly, opinionated. He knew that Shawn would rely on him to remain impartial. Actually, he had no idea who had promoted which projects, and he really preferred it that way.

It was Wednesday, about 3:00. He decided to do the additional work at home, so that it wouldn't interfere with his regular duties. He could also work without interruption and without 'influence' from upper managers. He paged Donna, his secretary. She looked up through the small window between their offices.

"Donna, I need you to collect some data for me. You should be able to talk to our staff accountants for most of it. The rest you can find on our last 10-K. Oh, and find out what our daily stock prices were for the last couple of months, both preferred and common."

Donna raised her eyebrow. "Planning a hostile takeover?" she asked.

"Do you really want to know? It concerns the meeting earlier today," Howard replied.

"No, I probably don't want to know," she replied. "What kind of information do you want from the staffers? I'll get that first."

"I need to know what five projects they're talking about, what the price tag is for each one, and what rate of return was estimated for each one. I want to go over their calculations, too, just to make sure they're perfect. I'll write down the rest of the information for you. You can pick it up when you get back. Thanks, Donna."

COMPANY BACKGROUND

Lehman Container Corporation started in Indianapolis in 1978, providing plastic injection-molded products to a wide variety of customers. The most popular product, by far, was plastic containers for food packaging and industrial uses. Virtually any size, color, and translucency could be delivered by Lehman. The company was not competitive with firms producing wide varieties of shapes for plastic products. Within their niche, however (round containers) Lehman could be considered the leading manufacturer, with three other firms running close behind.

Lehman experienced some reduction in the level of sales growth during the three recessions since 1978. Sales growth had not become negative, however, at any point since the company was founded. Many of Lehman's products were used as food containers or for chemicals and detergents. Although not recession-proof, the industry and the product demand seemed to have some immunity to economic downturns. The main key to success in the industry, it seemed, was to hold the leading competitive position.

INFORMATION COLLECTED ON THE PROJECTS

At home, Howard opened the box of materials Donna had collected during the day. He spread the materials on the desk in his home office. Donna had obviously outdone herself. She had copied the entire prospectus on each project - much more material than Howard needed. She had also downloaded a tremendous amount of market data on the firm's different securities. At least he had everything he needed to get started; that was better than wanting something he didn't have.

Howard decided to summarize the information he needed into tables. In college, he had gotten into the habit of typing thoughts as he worked. He turned on his computer and opened the spreadsheet program, and began summarizing the information. Howard's summaries appear in Exhibits 1,2, and 3.

All of the information would be useful in presenting alternative combinations of projects. Each combination, he decided, should also be analyzed according to any of three different ways of determining the firm's marginal cost of capital. Howard reached for his intermediate financial management text, which he had kept from college. "Hope this stuff hasn't changed much," he thought to himself. He reviewed the sections on cost of capital. It was just as he had recalled; there were three basic ways of considering cost of capital: discounted cash flow methods, using the CAPM (capital asset pricing model) to price equity, and using a rather subjective method called the 'bond yield plus risk premium' approach for pricing equity. After determining each component cost (debt, preferred equity, and common equity), he could just calculate weighted average costs to get an idea of the firm's overall cost of capital. This cost, in percent, could be directly compared to the returns on the projects.

Howard considered how much time he needed to allocate for the analysis. Shawn had sent him an email message that he would like to have the results by Friday afternoon's meeting. That gave Howard two nights to work on it. "Better get to work," he thought, and began entering the data into the spreadsheet.

Exhibit 1: Returns and Initial Costs.

PROJECT	IRR%	NET INITIAL COST
IBM Computing Facility	18.0	$1.78 million
Sun Microsystems Facility	17.4	$1.83 million
Curry Business Park Factory	21.2	$2.4 million
York Factory	20.6	$2.1 million
Molding Machinery Updates	16.8	$3.02 million

Exhibit 2: Market Information.

Average Price of Common Stock (recent levels)	$11.08
Average Price of Preferred Stock (recent levels)	$9.12 ($10 par)
Last Dividend (annual) on Common Stock	$1.01
Dividend (annual) on Preferred Stock	$1.00 (10% on par)
Flotation Costs on New Issues (per share)	$0.72
Lehman's Bond Yield	11%
Lehman's Secured Bank LOC (Max $1.5 million)	9%

5-year averages:

Average Return on Treasury Bills	2.8%
Average Return on Treasury Bond	4.2%
Average Return on a Broad Stock Market Index	13.1%
Risk Premium for BY+RP approach	7%

Exhibit 3: Financial Information.

Sales Growth (5-year)	8%
Earnings Growth (5-year)	4.5%
Earnings per Share Growth (5-year)	3.4%
Beta on Lehman stock	1.1
Current Marginal Tax Rate	34%
Available Retained Earnings	$706,000
Capitalization	38% debt
	6% pref. equity
	56% com. equity

LAURA'S SUMMARY OF THE MEETING

By Thursday afternoon, Laura had completed her transcription of positions expressed during the meeting on Wednesday. She had given it to Shawn in the form of a memo; only one page. Shawn paged her on the intercom. "Laura, on this memo. Is it really just a one-pager?"

"You told me to take out the profanity," she replied. "What is there is really all that got discussed during the meeting. There was some repetition, but the same views were expressed each time."

"OK, Laura, thanks. You DO seem to have captured the essence of everyone's positions. Why don't you send Ledbetter a copy?" "Done," Laura replied.

The memo appears in exhibit 4.

Exhibit 4: Summary of Executive Arguments.

MEMORANDUM

To: Shawn Weatherbee, CEO
From: Laura Witt, Executive Assistant
RE: Transcription: Summary of Sept. 1, 2004 Meeting
Date: September 2, 2004

A summary of expressed positions, organized by project, appears below.

IBM vs. SUN Computer Facility:
STAN: No opinion. Doesn't care whether the IBM or Sun System is used, as long as it gets the job done.

BOB: Strongly favors SUN system, because the current system is a SUN system, his personnel would not have a long period of orienting to a new brand. Claims it would be more cost effective to stay with SUN, because no retraining costs would arise. Also thinks IBM is an inferior product.

LEE: Strongly prefers IBM system, mainly because he feels it is a more efficient system with better technical support. Argues that the IBM offers more to extended purposes within the firm, such as better support of online business, and has promise for supporting a future office network, as well as serving manufacturing needs. Also thinks SUN is an inferior product.

York vs. Curry Business Park Location:
STAN: Strongly prefers York location because of access to transportation options (a port, rail, and road access). Feels that York local governments would welcome them and provide amiable environment. Dislikes Curry because of difficulty in distributing products and requirement that the firm sign a 40-year lease.

BOB: Strongly prefers Curry location because of its provision of acreage for waste product storage, provision of utilities services, and long-term lease (40 years). Dislikes York because of distance from home office and lack of acreage for waste products- claims it would not be cost effective to ship waste materials from the site frequently. Also feels that the York local governments would not be cooperative.

LEE: No preference.

Molding Machinery Updates:
STAN: Favors overhauling current equipment with the Molding Machinery Updates project. Realizes that the inefficiency of the existing machines has contributed to backlogs in the past. Strongly opposes new equipment as wasteful.

BOB: Strongly opposes updates or status quo. Feels that other managers have been ignoring the need for new equipment for several manufacturing pods. Thinks that keeping existing machines is a recipe for disaster. Strongly favors new equipment.

LEE: In favor of status quo. Nervous about possible downturn in the economy.

REQUIRED

1. Calculate component costs of capital and create graphs of the marginal cost of capital (MCC) for each of the methods in the case (DCF, CAPM, and BY+RP). Why is there no retained earnings breakpoint for the CAPM and BY+RP methods?

2. Create the Investment Opportunity Schedule for each of the four possible combinations of projects, bearing in mind which ones are mutually exclusive.

3. Determine the optimal capital budget. Remember that the nature of these projects rules out project divisibility.

Case 12

WORKING COMPUTERS, INC.

Jennifer Sobieski, an analyst in the headquarters of Working Computers, has been asked to evaluate whether or not Working should sell a division of the firm which has been losing market share and requires a great deal of new investment to remain competitive. The ailing product is a personal data appliance, or PDA, that once led the market in features and innovation, only to fall prey to competition from numerous firms once it had paved the way for the product category. Complicating Jennifer's analysis and recommendation are several political issues involving the wayward division. In particular, Working's recently returned CEO, Stewart Workman, has decided that the product (the Bernoulli device) is a "loser" and has plans to use the capital currently committed to Bernoulli to boost the ailing performance of other parts of the firm.

JENNIFER'S POSITION

In the jobs she worked throughout high school and college, Jennifer Sobieski had never encountered a corporate culture as intense and pervasive as the culture at Working Computers. The corporate motto, displayed on banners, T-shirts and coffee cups throughout the headquarters complex, was "Everyone here really believes in Working." On her long commute home, often after twelve-hour days in the office, she imagined that monks of the Dark Ages had faced a similar environment. Even though she was just a beginner, she could see that becoming part of the company was going to be as challenging to her social and political skills as it was to her technical background. Working Computers had a long history of internal struggle, and it had a loyal user base that had to be kept happy as well.

Jennifer had been hired as a marketing analyst, in accordance with the jobs she had worked during school. After several months, however, it was clear to her superiors that she was far more valuable as someone who could see the future and attach numbers to it. They had decided to promote her to the position of "Cost Engineer," which seemed to have a nice ring to it, and gave her a bigger cubical and more responsibility. Thankfully, the new "office" was also closer to the communal coffee machine. The new position was also more in line with her education; she had studied manufacturing technology, finance and industrial engineering in college, and she was putting much of that background to use every day.

Jennifer was struggling with the decision to divest (or perhaps eliminate) a currently profitable product line. Her immediate superior, Tom LaPonte, was the controller and chief financial officer for Working Computers, and had entrusted Jennifer with a super-secret question: could Working do without the Bernoulli division? To be sure, the ultimate decision would be made by LaPonte and the other executives of the firm, including the quixotic and visionary founder and CEO, Stewart Workman. Her task centered on developing the numbers necessary to portray all relevant aspects of the decision. In addition, she had a feeling that this project was one of special interest to the CEO.

WORKING COMPUTERS

Working Computers had been in business for almost thirty years, and it built and distributed a unique line of desktop computers, laptop computers, and an operating system which was preferred by media professionals around the world. In addition to traditional computers, Working had been one of the first companies to market what had come to be known as a "PDA" or personal data appliance. The research and development expenditure for that product line had come at a time when the company was facing stiff competition in the laptop and desktop markets, and millions of dollars had been spent creating a completely new and innovative interface for the Working PDA -- the Bernoulli device. Working's top management, at the time, had felt certain that personal computers were moving in the direction of smaller, more specialized computers which would perform a few tasks more conveniently than a traditional laptop.

THE BERNOULLI DEVICE

The Bernoulli device was a small, handheld device the size of a stenographer's pad with integrated applications for recording appointments, addresses and contact information, as well as freeform text notes. It had been designed to replace the traditional executive calendar binders that Jennifer and so many of her colleagues had carried in school, but it had evolved into much more than that. The Bernoulli had been popular due to the ability of users to write new software for the machines. Users had quickly learned that their investment in the Bernoulli gave them the option to program the machines for almost any task, from electronic reference books to data acquisition from industrial machines. Best of all, the Bernoulli would easily interface with a host computer for uploading and printing. The more recent incarnations of the device had been built for accessing Internet news services and email servers from the field without the need for a full-size laptop or host computer. For reliability, the Bernoulli had no moving parts.

With success, after a rocky start, came competition. Several different firms had developed PDAs which improved on aspects of the Bernoulli, even though the research and development folks at Working had tried to keep the device current. Most importantly, competitors sold machines which could be connected to a variety of different computing platforms; the Bernoulli device would only upload and download from a Working-brand computer. In addition, even with Working's head start, competitors had used manufacturers outside of the U.S. to lower production costs. To make matters worse, major software developers were beginning to support competing platforms at the expense of the Bernoulli, and that was taking its own toll on market share.

THE PRODIGAL SON RETURNS

Stewart Workman had recently returned to the firm after nearly ten years heading various other successful and unsuccessful companies. When the board of directors ousted him, he targeted his vision and energy towards developing an understanding of the future of computing. Workman had felt that computers could enhance the life of every consumer. He had anticipated the development of the Internet and the World Wide Web, and his interim firms had targeted the academic and research markets with these innovations in mind. In late 2003, however, Working Computers had been in trouble, and the board of directors decided that Workman might have the ability to "save the farm." With that in mind, they offered him the position of CEO and chairman of the board. Workman, already wealthy from his other ventures and his early investment in Working stock, accepted a salary of $10 per year for this role, and the board granted him an incentive plan that awarded stock options according to the growth of the company's stock price. With that type of encouragement, Workman began asserting his desire for innovation and market leadership, and cast a wary eye toward products and services where the firm was less than dominant.

Workman had already let it be known that he would be outsourcing much of the company's production, based on analyses that Sobieski and LaPonte had put together and backed up with hard numbers from Working's overseas partners. Stewart had also made it clear that the firm would take a different direction, one that stressed leadership in innovation and product design. In keeping with this approach, he had mentioned more that once that the Bernoulli device was "behind the times" and a "drain on the rest of the corporation." In fact, in one recent executive meeting which included the head of the Bernoulli division, Workman had referred to Bernoulli as a "black hole of creativity and internal funds." The board of directors had allowed Workman to commission research from LaPonte regarding the viability of Bernoulli as an ongoing product. In Workman's mind it was clear that the funds that currently went to Bernoulli could be put to use rebuilding the company's market share in desktop and laptop computers. Given the depressed state of the firm's stock price, which was at an all-time low, the board was desperate to find ways of regaining the popularity and reputation that the firm had once enjoyed.

JUST THE FACTS

Jennifer had discretely gathered a great deal of information from the Bernoulli unit as well as several of its competitors. In addition, she had spent the greater part of a week downloading information from the Internet, mainly opinions of the PDA market and the strengths and weaknesses of Bernoulli as an ongoing platform.

Jennifer thought that Bernoulli's declining market share was troublesome. In 2003, Bernoulli unit sales had represented approximately fifteen percent of the market, with the largest competitor grabbing a full 42 percent of unit sales. Unfortunately, market share had been declining at least one percent each quarter, and there was fear that it would drop even more. This drop was likely due to a large competitor's recent announcement that compatibility with its platform, and not the Bernoulli, would be incorporated into a popular line of office software that was unavailable for Working Computers.

The folks in the Bernoulli labs were currently working on major upgrades to the Bernoulli device as well as the Bernoulli interface software; these improvements would make Bernoulli compatible with almost every personal computer on the market. To continue this research, the Bernoulli division estimated that it would need no less than $18 million in the next month in order to finish the development of the more advanced product. Allocating this investment within the division was the responsibility of the division's operating officer, and Jennifer was confident that the money would be put to good use. When the new products became available in late 2004, it was likely that Bernoulli could regain as much as 8 percent of the market within the first year, with gains of four percent per year after that. Nonetheless, in recent meetings, Stewart Workman had criticized the $18 million request as being "insane," stating that he knew of several places in the company where those funds could "earn at least our normal cost of capital for the shareholders." The firm had enough cash available for this type of investment, but Jennifer reasoned that Workman was taking the allocation of that money personally. Jennifer had forecasted unit sales for the periods 2004 through 2009 (Exhibit 1), and she had calculated demand both with and without the additional market share that the new product was expected to generate.

Exhibit 1.

Working Computers
Unit Sales Projections
Periods ending December 31, 2003 through December 31, 2009
(units, in thousands)

	12/31/03	12/31/04	12/31/05	12/31/06	12/31/07	12/31/08	12/31/09
Units Sold, with new investment	180,000	150,000	189,000	246,000	264,000	264,000	264,000
Units Sold, without new investment	180,000	150,000	102,000	57,000	48,000	48,000	48,000

Currently, the Bernoulli division operated with a cost of goods sold of approximately sixty percent of the unit price and operating expenses (excluding depreciation) averaging 24 percent of total revenues. The division expected to sell a total of 300,000 units by the end of 2003 at a price of $495 each. The model expected to ship beginning in late 2004 would sell at the same price point. The division's managers estimated, though, that the revised Bernoulli would have a cost of goods sold of 54 percent of the retail price with higher operating expenses of 26 percent due to increased advertising. Given the competitive nature of the industry, this price point and cost estimate were expected to remain the same for the next several years.

For strategic planning purposes, Working's management allocated depreciation to the existing Bernoulli division as though the entire division was an asset in the modified accelerated cost recovery (MACRS) 10-year class, with five years of operation behind it. The initial investment of $56 million had been made in early 1999. Recovery allowance percentages according to MACRS are shown in Exhibit 2. The new funds allocated to the division would be treated similarly, except that management had decided that any new investment would be depreciated using the MACRS category for 5-year assets; due to changes in the industry since 1999, this was expected to be more consistent with the nature of the market for computing devices and PDAs. Working's managers used a weighted average cost of capital, or hurdle rate, of 14.5 percent when evaluating capital budgeting projects, and Jennifer felt that this would be an appropriate discount rate in this instance as well. The firm's marginal tax rate, for planning purposes, was 34 percent.

Finally, Jennifer had to consider the fact that the company always held the option to sell the Bernoulli division to an existing competitor. In fact, there were rumors on the Internet that several quiet and unofficial offers had already been discussed with the members of the board of directors. In developing her analysis, Jennifer would have to come up with an estimate of a price for the division, based on the sales and market share expectations she had gathered. To establish a terminal value in the final forecast year, 2009, she would capitalize the cash flows in that year by dividing them by Working's overall cost of capital, essentially treating that year's cash flow as the payment from a perpetuity. In the event that management declined to invest the requested $18 million today, the Bernoulli division could still maintain some level of sales for several years, and the patents held by the division would be worth selling or licensing as well.

Exhibit 2.
Modified Accelerated Cost Recovery (MACRS) Allowance Percentages

Ownership Year	5-year assets	10-year assets
1	20%	10%
2	32%	18%
3	19%	14%
4	12%	12%
5	11%	9%
6	6%	7%
7		7%
8		7%
9		7%
10		6%
11		3%

For her previous presentations to senior management, Jennifer had produced detailed discounted cash flow analyses accompanied by documents to support her assumptions. In addition, she usually spent some time developing sensitivity analyses using any numbers that she expected to be questioned by the board. This time, her main fear was that her understanding of the growth in market share, because of the revised Bernoulli due in late 2004, would turn out to be optimistic.

After reviewing her notes, Jennifer grabbed her gym bag and headed off to the fitness center in the next building. She anticipated having a long night ahead of her, and a jog and a shower was just the thing to clear her head and help her focus. Once in the lobby of her building, she passed under several hanging banners promoting the company's newest products, bearing slogans such as "Imagine Working" and "We're Working For You." Another read "We're Always Working" in the corporation's trademarked font. Reading this banner, Jennifer slowed and said to herself, "Isn't that the truth."

REQUIRED

1. Given the unit sales information in Exhibit 1, develop an annual revenue forecast for 2004 through 2009. Forecast sales first assuming that the revised Bernoulli will be introduced one year from today, and then create a forecast which is based on sales of the current model, assuming that Working declines to invest more capital in Bernoulli.

2. Use the cost information Jennifer has assembled to construct a forecast of cost of goods sold and operating expenses for 2004 through 2009. Assume first that the Bernoulli will be introduced, with its new cost structure, one year from now, and then calculate a cost forecast assuming that the $18 million is not provided for development of the new product.

3. Using the information developed for Questions 1 and 2, develop a discounted cash flow analysis for the Bernoulli division for 2004 through 2009. Working's board has asked for net present value and internal rate of the return when making decisions in the past. Complete your analysis assuming that the additional investment is contributed today. Be sure to recognize a terminal value for the division at the end of 2009.

4. Make a recommendation as to whether or not Working Computers should contribute the requested $18 million to the Bernoulli. Be sure to recognize all aspects of the decision, including the potential impact that the requested ongoing investment dollars could have on the plans of Stewart Workman.

5. Jennifer expects Stewart Workman to ask about selling the Bernoulli division. What price should Working ask for if it sells Bernoulli today, immediately after making the requested investment? What price could it expect to receive if it plans to leave Bernoulli alone?

6. In addition to the issues in Questions 1 through 5, what other considerations might be appropriate when a firm is considering eliminating a product line or divesting a division?

Case 13

AUTOMOTIVE SPECIALTIES, INCORPORATED

Automotive Specialties, Incorporated (ASI) is a domestic division of a multinational holding company, and it has been invited by its largest customer (also a large multinational firm) to build a new plant in the small South American country of Mesa Verde. Jamie Miles, assistant treasurer of ASI, has reviewed the customer's proposal and she has developed several analyses and forecasts of her own to supplement that information. Although most of the uncertainty of foreign investment will be handled through the liason with ASI's customer, Fujimora Transport, the value of the investment hasn't yet been determined. In addition, the customer may have motives that the management of ASI will need to consider before committing funds to such an ambitious project.

INTRODUCTION

With so many deadlines and fires to fight, Jamie Miles saw no end to her day. She had grown to love her job, and especially the title of "Assistant Treasurer", but no amount of amour or prestige could smooth over the eyestrain or hasty lunches in the company canteen. In obtaining the title of Assistant Treasurer, and the fancy business cards that came with it, Jamie had worked ninety-hour weeks for as long as she could remember. Holidays were just something noted on a calendar; they were days when she could work uninterrupted by phone calls. She could remember her last year of school, and how things had seemed so tough then. After a six-month job search, endless interviews, and a year on the job, the last couple of semesters' of work toward her finance degree seemed to have been another life entirely. She had no doubt that the next few weeks would be more intense, yet, as she helped prepare the capital budget for the upcoming year.

Most of the projects that crossed her desk were routine replacements of existing equipment or expansions of product lines into new markets. The project that was giving her the most trouble, this week, involved the decision to enter into an agreement to open a plant offshore. One of her best customers, Fujimora Transport, operated several assembly plants in South America. Fujimora had proposed that Automotive Specialties build a new plant adjacent to one of the Fujimora facilities in an effort to streamline inventory management and reduce costs. In fact, the proposal from Fujimora guaranteed funding of the operation at a reasonable cost of capital, promised to secure the legal (and political) arrangements, and

91

included compensation for training and personnel services for local workers who would be hired to operate the machines at the new plant. In addition, Fujimora had agreed that the facility should have a large enough capacity to allow Automotive Specialties to not only meet the current and future needs of Fujimora, but also to allow the company to expand its customer base in the region. Automotive Specialties' board of directors had agreed to fund a site survey and had commissioned Jamie to investigate the proposition prior to making a final commitment.

AUTOMOTIVE SPECIALTIES

Automotive Specialties, Incorporated (ASI) had existed in one form or another since the 1930s. It was a division of a larger firm, Stevens-Simper, Incorporated. Stevens-Simper had been around almost as long, and currently had operations in twelve other countries, with products and services ranging from automotive parts (with ASI) to underwater salvage and recovery. ASI was a small part of the conglomerate, and it was allowed to pursue opportunities each year and develop markets as its managers saw fit. The parent firm helped with raising capital and set targets for shareholder returns, but it left ASI to make most investment decisions independently. In fact, Jamie often used her counterparts in the "home office" as unofficial audiences for upcoming proposals for ASI's board, and the Stevens-Simper treasurer's office had provided a great deal of wisdom and expertise on many occasions.

ASI "specialized" in powdered metal fabrication. The firm mixed various types of metals in powdered form, pressed this powder into engine components, and then used skilled machine operators to finish the products into completed units. ASI's advantage was a patented process for pressing and sintering the products. In most cases, the resulting gears or cams would have little need for costly finishing labor. Because ASI refused to license this technology, the firm enjoyed a lower cost of production than most of its competitors. In addition, ASI products were often of much higher quality than the next best alternative. Given the company's research and expertise in the area, and the continuing refinements being made to the process, it was expected to continue this lead under its patent protection for the next five to eight years, at a minimum.

Fujimora had relied on ASI products for the past ten years, and sales to Fujimora represented almost 40 percent of ASI's annual revenue. ASI components were used in Fujimora products around the world, and ASI continually won praise and production bonuses from the firm. Many of the ASI executives and production staff had traveled to Japan to train and enjoy the hospitality of their best customer, and the relationship continued to develop as successive quarters of record output and quality went by. To be sure, ASI would continue to be a major supplier of components to Fujimora regardless of the decision to expand the smaller firm's facilities overseas.

MESA VERDE

The new plant was to be built in Mesa Verde, a small country located on the west coast of South America. Although many of its neighbors had experienced turbulent political situations in the recent past, Mesa Verde had been lucky. The country was a representative republic, with many of its laws and customs influenced by its trade with the US and Britain over the past thirty years. The current president had been in power for several years, and the country had enjoyed the right to elect its government for almost two generations. Due to its geographic isolation, the mountainous country had avoided conflicts with neighboring states as well. The resulting stability had allowed Mesa Verde to develop the infrastructure and human capital to support many diverse industries. In addition, Mesa Verde's diplomatic relationships with the developing markets of Brazil and Argentina provided opportunities for local firms to compete and reinvest their earnings in their homeland. Mesa Verde wasn't a perfect location, but it was one of the safest places that ASI could invest overseas. With Fujimora's backing and reputation in Mesa Verde, Jamie felt that ASI was being given a terrific opportunity.

ASI - MESA VERDE

The proposed plant would produce powdered metal products, initially, to meet the demand of the Fujimora plant in Mesa Verde. Currently, the Fujimora plant there ordered approximately ten percent of its purchases from ASI's domestic operation, with the remaining needs of the plant being met by small local shops or other offshore facilities. The Fujimora proposal was based on hiring and training many of the firm's local suppliers for work at the new ASI operation. Jamie had reviewed the expected demand quantities in the proposal and developed her own estimates of unit demand at the Mesa Verde plant (Exhibit I). In the table, Jamie listed the expected Fujimora demand for each product as "Mesa Verde" and eventual sales to other firms and/or markets as "other markets."

Exhibit 1. Expected Demand for Powdered Metal Products
ASI - Mesa Verde Plant
(annual units, in thousands)

Product	2006	2007	2008	2009	2010	2011
SKU 517						
Mesa Verde	155.10	160.60	167.00	173.70	181.07	189.18
other markets				43.43	45.27	47.30
SKU 453						
Mesa Verde	172.51	179.76	187.74	196.51	206.16	216.78
other markets				49.13	51.54	54.93
SKU 367a						
Mesa Verde	121.55	125.78	129.65	134.10	139.22	145.10
other markets				44.70	46.41	48.37

After reviewing the domestic cost estimates, Jamie thought that the current cost of goods sold allowance for each Mesa Verde product was close to the projected cost at the new plant, but she decided that she would need to lower the cost of labor factored into each. Currently, the cost of producing SKU 517, domestically, was approximately 67 percent of its unit selling price; in Mesa Verde, this would likely be lowered by twenty percent, to approximately 53.6 percent of the selling price. For SKU 453 and SKU 367a, the reduction would be similar, but these products had domestic costs of goods sold of 70 percent and 62 percent, respectively. In addition to reductions in cost, though, the firm would have to lower unit prices to accomodate Fujimora's wishes, and Jamie had compiled a listing of revised prices (adjusted for local inflation) in order to get an estimate of revenues for the proposed plant (Exhibit 2). Her numbers were based on her own research regarding the Mesa Verde economy, current and historical exchange rate trends, and the political history of monetary policy in the small country. The official currency of Mesa Verde was the royale, and it had enjoyed remarkable stability against the U.S. dollar in recent years. Because the Mesa Verde operation would be trading with other currencies which were not as strong, Jamie estimated prices for exports in royales as well.

Exhibit 2. Expected Unit Prices for Powdered Metal Products
ASI - Mesa Verde Plant

Product	2006	2007	2008	2009	2010	2011
SKU 517						
U.S. price	$10.75	$11.13	$11.52	$11.92	$12.34	$12.77
Mesa Verde	R860	R868.14	R875.52	R882.08	R888.48	R893.90
SKU 453						
U.S. price	$11.17	$11.67	$12.20	$12.75	$13.32	$13.92
Mesa Verde	R893.60	R910.26	R927.20	R943.50	R959.04	R974.40
SKU 367a						
U.S. price	$20.67	$21.39	$22.14	$22.92	$23.72	$24.55
Mesa Verde	R1,653.60	R1668.42	R1682.64	R1695.08	R1707.84	R1718.50

Current estimates of operating expenses were approximately ten percent of per-unit prices, domestically, and this was expected to increase to sixteen percent in Mesa Verde in the first two years of the new plant's operation. Jamie expected operating costs to decrease by 2007 to an estimated 13.5 percent of unit price, and the Fujimora estimates agreed with this, more or less.

According to both the Fujimora proposal and the engineer's report on her desk, the plant would cost approximately $11.6 million to build (beginning immediately), and it could be in operation at the end of the next calendar year (2005). It would require an additional working capital outlay of approximately $1.2 million, which wouldn't be needed until the start of operations in early 2006. The engineer's report and site survey had already cost the firm $100,000 in the prior quarter.

Even though Fujimora had agreed to secure financing for the project, Jamie's contacts at Stevens-Simper had suggested that she use the allocated weighted-average cost of capital that ASI used for domestic projects when discounting the Mesa Verde proposal. Currently, that hurdle rate was set at 10.95 percent. Jamie had considered adjusting the hurdle rate for the extra risk inherent when investing in emerging markets, but her advisors warned against this, suggesting that she apply any risk adjustments to the cash flows instead. Depending upon her assessment of the political risk of the investment, Jamie knew that she could always adjust each annual cash flow (after taxes) downward by some amount. Due to the safe economic and political environment of Mesa Verde, Jamie didn't plan on adjusting cash flows for political risk. In addition, she had already adjusted her demand estimates for uncertainty.

Her advisors also suggested that any risk stemming from expected fluctuations in the overall economy and exchange rates should be incorporated into Jamie's projection of exchange rates. Jamie planned to address this type of risk by completing analyses of several different scenarios which would illustrate the uncertainty of the cash flows from the Mesa Verde project due to a weakening royale. As for her sales estimates, Jamie felt certain that Fujimora would stand ready to purchase the necessary units of each SKU from domestic production in the event that the Mesa Verde operation proved untenable. After all, this plant had been Fujimora's idea in the first place!

One of Jamie's friends at the "home office" had suggested, quietly, that Fujimora would offer to purchase the ASI operation at the end of Jamie's planning horizon of six years. Most likely, the firm could negotiate with Fujimora to obtain a fair price, or one which would at least cover ASI's investment in the plant. Jamie would calculate a "terminal value" for the plant in 2011 based upon treating the annual cash flow in that year as a perpetuity. To value that cash flow stream, she had decided to use the firm's cost of capital as a rough approximation of the required return on such a perpetuity. Because the project will be sold as a complete operation in the final year, the working capital contribution would not be recovered in the final period. In addition, the revenues earned in Mesa Verde would be subject to the local marginal tax rate of 45 percent, and ASI could depreciate the initial investment over the six year period using the straight-line method approved for corporations in Mesa Verde. Under the current U.S. tax code and several treaties, profits from Mesa Verde wouldn't be subjected to additional corporate taxes once they were brought back into the country by ASI.

By the time Jamie had reviewed this information and summarized her notes for the board, it would be well past her normal lunch hour. She stood and walked to the office door, opening it and noticing her name and title stenciled on the frosted glass. As she headed to the canteen, yet again, she thought about the Mesa Verde plant and wondered when she would get to see it for herself. How often did assistant treasurers get to go on fact-finding missions?

REQUIRED

1. Using the demand and price estimates in Exhibits 1 and 2, develop annual revenue projections for the Mesa Verde project.

2. Using the information in the case, develop estimates of the cost of goods sold for each SKU, operating costs, and depreciation expense for the Mesa Verde plant for each of the next six years.

3. According to the budgeted figures calculated for Questions 1 and 2, produce a discounted cash flow analysis for the Mesa Verde project. Include estimates of the project's net present value and internal rate of return. Express the annual cash flows and net present value in dollars, according to Jamie's estimate of the royale-to-dollar exchange rate. (According to the numbers in Exhibit 2, the estimated exchange rate today and in 2006 will be R80 per dollar, and this is expected to appreciate by R2 each year afterwards.) Should ASI accept the project?

4. Jamie's initial estimates assume that the royale will strengthen over the next several years. Reproduce the analysis asked for in Questions 1 through 3 to reflect the possibility that the royale will weaken (by R2 per year) against the dollar over the project's planning horizon. Should the new plant be built?

5. Jamie consulted several economists and the World Wide Web and found that the chance of the royale weakening (in the manner described in Question 4) is approximately 38 percent. Calculate the project's expected net present value and internal rate of return using this additional information. How should this impact Jamie's recommendation?

6. What other considerations should ASI make when deciding upon the Mesa Verde investment?

SECTION 5

LEVERAGE AND RISK

Case 14

GILAD PUBLISHING COMPANY

Annette Gilad, general manager of Gilad Publishing Company (GPC), is faced with a decision point in the life of the company. Recently, an expansion in GPC publications has necessitated the purchase of new equipment and perhaps the addition of new personnel. Annette's decisions will significantly impact the risk and profitability prospects for GPC's future.

BACKGROUND

Gilad Publishing Company (GPC) is a small publisher located in Memphis, Tennessee. GPC serves a growing market for publishing soft and hard-bound books and periodicals. GPC mainly serves the market for specialty educational books, small-run company publications (such as catalogs), and books that are not expected to sell large quantities in bookstores (called "specialties"). The firm has the reputation of being a small company that has achieved competitiveness in both the pricing of specific jobs and in the effective marketing of specialty publications. The company has limited its publishing to physical book production and marketing. The virtual (electronic) publishing arena appears to be beyond GPC's capabilities and is not an area involving their competitive advantages. GPC also has avoided trying to compete with large publishers because of pricing disadvantages and higher per-unit costs. Fortunately, these large publishers are not particularly interested in smaller jobs that GPC can easily handle.

GPC deals with customers in two distinct ways. For 'custom publishing' customers desiring to either market their product themselves or who seek GPC's services for printing and bookbinding, the firm will submit bids based on cost coverage plus an acceptable markup. Other customers approach GPC for the purpose of manuscript evaluation, and upon acceptance, marketing of their works (acquisitions). The manner with which GPC deals with each scenario is very different.

Lewis Alcorn is associate manager in charge of the acquisitions division. He decides which manuscripts are worthy of publication and marketing, and oversees the process from selection to delivery (to book retailers). Lewis considers himself an 'underwriter' of sorts since the company takes the risk (concerning future sales) resulting from his decisions about manuscript submissions. Lewis considers a book that meets or exceeds sales expectations a 'winner' and ones that fail to meet these expectations 'losers.' This is almost always a self-fulfilling prophecy, since Lewis's pricing methodology is based on expected product sales.

Tammy Lange manages GPC's other division, custom publishing. Tammy deals with customers desiring to have their own work published and sometimes marketed. Custom publishing differs from acquisitions in that the custom publishing customer bears the initial or the entire cost of production. Under this arrangement, GPC incurs little risk, since payment is received in advance. There exists the possibility for incremental income, though, from a markup on all units sold beyond an established minimum paid for by the customer.

COST STRUCTURE DECISIONS

GPC's general manager, Annette Gilad, started the company in 1991. She has taken the firm from its infancy with only four acquired titles and ten custom publishing accounts to its current levels. The firm now has 830 titles and 2,390 active custom publishing customers. With its initial purchase of equipment in 1991, only marginal investment in additional equipment has occurred in the past eleven years. Now Annette faces a relatively severe need for additional capacity; a situation calling for considerable fundraising. GPC has had to 'farm out' some of its projects to bookbinding services in the area, simply because lengthier production runs tended to outstrip GPC's production capacity. This had adversely affected GPC's profit margin, which was traditionally in the 10-15% range, but had shrunk to about 3%, since some of the farmed out projects had higher costs than GPC could recover with revenues. These larger jobs were becoming too numerous, and the profit potential was negative if the work was contracted with other bookbinding services. This convinced Annette that a larger, modern production facility would solve these issues.

GPC is a private corporation, and is closely held by the Gilad family in Memphis. Annette has already found another investor willing to assume a minority shareholder position, holding 20% of the firm's stock. To make the stock attractive to the new shareholder, the Gilad family shareholders all agreed to forego dividend receipts on their shares for two years. The new shareholder also agreed to receive dividends as 30% of positive net income, relieving GPC of the burden of dividend expense if earnings were low or negative. The new investor will receive 200,000 shares of GPC stock for a price of $60 per share. GPC will receive $12 million from the sale, less a 1% fee for legal and other related costs. The new shareholder agreed to reduce the total amount to be invested if Annette decided that less was necessary. One condition, however, was that at least 100,000 shares would be available at the $60 price. Annette's only alternative to raising between $6 and $12 million in equity was not to raise equity funds at all. This would cause the entire amount of any expansion to be financed with debt.

Although the investor seemed inflexible, Annette was willing to bend, because she had experienced difficulty finding an equity investor at all, given the fact that the investor would basically be a minority shareholder in a family owned corporation. She realized that this was not a very attractive position for an equity investor. The fact that someone was willing, even with the constraints, was unusual.

Annette has secured a letter of intent from a large bank in the area for up to $3 million. The equipment would involve an equipment mortgage on all of the new equipment purchased, not just the portion purchased directly with borrowed funds. A lower interest rate could be obtained on the loan if the value of the pledged assets exceeds the balance on the loan by a wide margin. The equipment will be fully depreciated by the end of the tenth year, although estimates of useful productive life are almost 20 years. Payments would be monthly on the ten-year loan, and the bank has offered a competitive 8.75% fixed rate of interest.

The bank requires that GPC specify the portion of the approved financing they need by the end of the current month. In order to specify a borrowing need for the fixed assets involved in the expansion, Annette needs to decide on one of the possible operational/financing alternatives, outlined below. In the event that GPC needs more funding than provided by the bank for the expansion, the additional amount will have to be raised.

OPERATIONAL ALTERNATIVES

Two proposals have been forwarded by GPC's cost accountant as alternative ways of structuring operations. They each involve differing levels of investment in fixed assets, and thus differing levels of other productive inputs. Annette asked that all operating expenses be identified as fixed or variable (with respect to sales levels). A summary of costs under each of the three proposals appears in Exhibit 1.

Exhibit 1: Operational Alternatives.

FULL EXPANSION ($16,000,000 investment in fixed assets)

Additional Annual Revenues and Operating Costs:

Revenues	$21,600,000
Fixed Cost	$4,000,000
Variable Cost	$200,000

PARTIAL EXPANSION (B) ($8,000,000 investment in fixed assets)

Additional Annual Revenues and Operating Costs:

Revenues	$9,800,000
Fixed Cost	$2,048,000
Variable Cost	$ 156,000

*Direct Costs are assumed to remain at the same percent of sales
**Tax rate is a constant 32%
***Depreciation is straight line with a ten year asset life, and is included in fixed costs.

Exhibit 2: Income Statement for the year ended December 31, 2003.

Net Sales (Titles)	$16,600,000.00	
Net Sales (Custom Publishing)	4,790,000.00	
Total Net Sales		21,390,000.00
Expenses:		
Direct Materials Cost (Titles)	-8,843,000.00	
Direct Materials Cost (Custom Publishing)	-4,124,000.00	
Total Direct Materials Cost		-12,967,000.00
Variable Operating Costs	-6,320,000.00	
Total Fixed Costs	-1,006,000.00	
Total Operating Cost		-7,326,000.00
Earnings Before Interest and Taxes		1,097,000.00
Interest Expense	-102,000.00	
Tax Expense	-372,980.00	
NET INCOME		$622,020.00

Exhibit 3: Balance Sheet. December 31, 2003.

Current Assets:		
Cash and Equivalents	$91,000.00	
Accounts Receivable	818,000.00	
Inventory	3,301,000.00	
Prepaid Items	109,000.00	
Total Current Assets		4,319,000.00
Fixed Assets		4,102,000.00
TOTAL ASSETS		$8,421,000.00
Liabilities:		
Accounts Payable	$898,000.00	
Short-Term Loan	12,000.00	
Bonds Payable	1,000,000.00	
Total Liabillities		1,910,000.00
Equity:		
Common Stock	2,000,000.00	
Retained Earnings	4,511,000.00	
Total Equity		6,511,000.00
TOTAL LIABILITIES + EQUITY		$8,421,000.00

REQUIRED

1. Which of the firm's divisions is more risky, and why? In terms of size, comment on each of the expansion plans. Would a creditor be concerned? Why?

2. Estimate income statements for 2003 for each of the two expansion scenarios. Assume that Annette wants to minimize the amount invested by the equity investor, preferring to use debt for financing as much as she can. Remember to consider the investor's requirements.

3. Estimate the 2004 DOL, DFL, and DCL for the firm, for each expansion. Does it appear from the resulting earnings that it is advisable for GPC to favor high leverage?

4. What are the implications of higher depreciation concerning 1) cashflow and 2) fixed charge coverage?

5. Now assume that Annette will maximize use of common stock financing for all expansions, up to the limits that the new investor has asserted. How does this change your answer in number 3? (consider that common stock has a flexible cash payment, and that it typically involves a higher required return by investors)

6. What is the implication of stockholders giving up current income?

SECTION 6

COST OF CAPITAL

Case 15

SCOPE CITY, INCORPORATED (A)

There was little time in Ruby Damodaran's day for casual chatting, but every time her boss came by she made the time. The CFO of Scope City, Tom Dillon, was her boss but he was also a great storyteller and a terrific source of information about the industry in which she had chosen to work.

Scope City, Incorporated (SCI) was a manufacturer, reseller and importer of advanced optical equipment, including consumer (amateur) telescopes, nautical optics, and accessories. Over the past thirty years the firm had grown from a small repair shop in east Texas to a regional leader in quality optical products. SCI's retail and catalog operations were known for friendly service and quick turnaround, and the firm's ability to repair even the most obscure instruments made them somewhat unique. After an initial public offering several years before, Scope City's shares traded regionally, and benefited from the company's reputation with its customers. Although the firm was still considered to be closely-held by most analysts, several national investment houses had begun to monitor the stock and tout the shares to institutional clients.

Tom Dillon was busy preparing Ruby to help him outline Scope City's prospects to potential shareholders at a regional "investors' conference" in a few weeks. Over three days, Scope City's team would have a chance to offer a presentation for institutional investors, first in a general setting with other small firms and then in individual sessions with specific investors, advisors and analysts. Tom's casual information sessions with Ruby were designed to build her background knowledge of the company and industry as rapidly as possible.

THANK YOU COMET HALLEY

As many folks in the telescope industry conceded, most consumers only became interested in watching the sky when there was some special event taking place. In the 1980s, the return of Comet Halley had been such an event. Amateur telescopes were sold in tremendous numbers in order to allow people to observe the great comet from their backyards, and media attention on the event prompted schools and universities to reopen visiting hours at observatories and promote scientific endeavors directly to the public. For

Scope City, struggling as a repair shop and reseller, it had been a great opportunity to grow, and Dillon and the other founders had spent more of their time running the business than looking skyward.

The several years immediately following the comet craze had proven to be lean ones for many optics firms, but Scope City's diverse customer base had given it a great advantage over its competitors. Even today, SCI had enough repair and wholesale business to allow it to remain profitable throughout the year, and it had a reputation sufficient to give it an advantage when the Christmas retail season arrived. In addition, SCI was the sole U.S. importer for several different optics manufacturers in Taiwan and Japan.

Each month SCI held free seminars at its stores to educate consumers on the value of quality optics and tried to help customers avoid the temptation to buy cheaper, mass-produced "department store" telescopes and binoculars. Although such telescopes were fairly common (and inexpensive) during the last few months of the year, most serious amateurs agreed that someone new to the hobby could easily be discouraged if the newcomer's introduction to the night sky was marred by an instrument of poor quality and workmanship. For the store staff, it was also a frustrating occasion when customers came in for help after spending several hundred dollars elsewhere -- there was only so much one could do to fix a poor design. The SCI staff and management felt that education was the best method for building their customer base, and these efforts had been repaid over time. SCI had also been a pioneer in using the Internet to provide information to consumers. The firm's free publication "A Beginner's Guide to Skywatching" was very popular at astronomy clubs and star parties around the country.

FINANCING THE STARS

As a recent finance graduate, Ruby Damodaran was new to the company, and she welcomed Dillon's insight and history lessons. It was imperative that she learn as much about SCI as possible before meeting with investors. Even though she didn't plan to spend much time at the podium, she knew that the success of SCI's presentation depended upon everyone on the team. She also knew that part of her role as assistant controller would be to make presentations of this type throughout the year and to be able to discuss the prospects of the firm when necessary. These days she was definitely in "study mode."

Ruby was currently struggling to get her conference agenda prepared, and also to make constructive comments about the material prepared by Dillon. One task that remained before the investors' conference was to examine the firm's current and expected growth and capital structure. She knew that Dillon and the other members of the board of directors didn't consider capital structure to be an important issue, but their discussions about the upcoming investors' conference had highlighted the need for new capital and innovative financing for future projects and potential acquisitions. In order to understand the need for any future financing, Ruby felt that she would need to understand the firm's capital up to this point. She had compiled the most recent balance sheet (Exhibit 1) and revenue figures (Exhibit 2), and collected some information regarding other aspects of the financing decision (Exhibit 3).

Exhibit 1. Scope City, Incorporated Balance Sheet. December 31, 2003.
(dollars, in thousands)

Current Assets	$5,625
Fixed Assets	$5,625
Total Assets	$11,250
Current Liabilities	$1,500
Long-Term Debt	$2,250
Common Stock ($2 par value)	$1,500
Retained Earnings	$6,000
Total Liab. & Equity	$11,250

Exhibit 2. Scope City, Incorporated. Revenue and Earnings.

Year	Sales	Net Income	EPS
1994	$7,500,000	$900,000	$1.20
1995	$10,312,500	$1,267,500	$1.69
1996	$12,000,000	$1,440,000	$1.92
1997	$18,750,000	$2,156,250	$2.88
1998	$21,375,000	$2,250,000	$3.00
1999	$23,250,000	$2,673,750	$3.57
2000	$27,375,000	$3,011,250	$4.02
2001	$31,875,000	$3,225,000	$4.30
2002	$34,125,000	$3,375,000	$4.50
2003	$38,625,000	$3,422,700	$4.56

Exhibit 3. Selected Capital Market, Firm & Industry Data.

Yield on AAA corporate debt	6%
Yield on 10-year U.S. Treasury bonds	5.10%
Historical average return on a broad market average of common stock	16%
Dividend payout ratio (average) for competitors in retail optics and repair	25%
Marginal tax rate for SCI (recent)	30%
Coupon rate, SCI's outstanding long-term debt	7.50%
Remaining term to maturity, SCI's outstanding long-term debt	6 years
Dividend payout ratio, SCI (recent)	32%
Market price per share, SCI (recent)	$18.00

SCI had recently been approached by the parent company of one of its smaller competitors, a specialized telescope manufacturing firm. It seemed that the directors of the parent firm, a holding company, were tired of trying to understand the telescope business and were ready to divest. Although these talks were going on in strict secrecy, SCI had participated in similar spin-offs in the past, and it was reasonable to include alternatives such as this one in the firm's plans for the future. The board of SCI didn't yet have a clear understanding of how or when this potential acquisition might take place, but they understood it's potential significance for the future of the company.

Ruby was concerned that institutional investors would want to know about the firm's alternatives and costs when determining its potential for growth. Ruby could remember from her finance classes that the firm's costs of capital were important considerations, but she had yet to take the time to put everything together. As the conference date approached, she also wanted to take some time to observe the heavens through several different SCI telescopes before leaving on her trip, in order to become more familiar with the products. "Perhaps after work tonight," she thought. After all, early morning was always a good time to go outside with a telescope.

REQUIRED

1. Describe the company's core business and the markets that it serves.

2. What are the compound average annual rates of growth for SCI's revenue and net income? How should the firm (eventually) analyze the value of the potential acquisition in light of these numbers?

3. What is SCI's historical (book) cost of equity?

4. What is SCI's historical (book) cost of long-term debt?

5. How do the firm's current liabilities influence the cost of capital calculation?

6. Using your answers for 3, 4 and 5 above, determine SCI's historical weighted-average cost of capital (WACC).

7. How should the presentation for the investors' conference discuss the firm's growth and historical cost of capital? How are historical costs relevant when discussing future investment?

8. What other information should Ruby Damodaran have on hand for her presentation to the conference? Additionally, what types of questions will investors likely ask of SCI? How will new types of investors (institutions, for example) likely impact SCI's choices of capital and strategy in the future?

Case 16

SCOPE CITY, INCORPORATED (B)

Ruby Damodaran had finally gotten a chance to spend some time outside with a couple of her company's premiere telescopes. She had carved out a few hours in the early winter morning to appreciate the night sky and the wonders that it offered. In addition, she had been able to familiarize herself with the product attributes that made customers so happy with their Scope City products.

Scope City, Incorporated (SCI) was a popular regional firm specializing in the manufacture, repair and distribution of nautical and consumer telescopes and binoculars. It had begun many years before as a repair company, and had grown in recent years to become the exclusive U.S. distributor of several popular lines of professional telescopes. At an upcoming conference of institutional investors, SCI would have an opportunity to discuss its products and future with a host of potential shareholders.

Ruby Damodaran, and her boss Tom Dillon, CFO of Scope City, were hustling to finish their presentations for the conference. In addition, they were faced with the opportunity to purchase the assets of one of SCI's competitors (the negotiations were being conducted in secrecy for the time being), and the firm's board of directors was contemplating sources of capital for this potential acquisition and the growth of the firm in general. It would be Ruby's task to make sure that the firm's presentations at the conference demonstrated SCI's value as a long-term investment.

In preparing her documents, Ruby had investigated the book value capital structure of the company. She began with the firm's most recent balance sheet, from the end of 2003 (Exhibit 1) and a history of the company's earnings and sales figures (Exhibit 2). Her current task was to develop an understanding of SCI's marginal cost of capital and the various sources of debt and equity available to the company.

Exhibit 1. Scope City, Incorporated. Balance Sheet, December 31, 2003.

(dollars, in thousands)

Current Assets	$5,625
Fixed Assets	$5,625
Total Assets	$11,250
Current Liabilities	$1,500
Long-Term Debt	$2,250
Common Stock ($2 par value)	$1,500
Retained Earnings	$6,000
Total Liab. & Equity	$11,250

Exhibit 2. Scope City, Incorporated. Revenue and Earnings.

Year	Sales	Net Income	EPS
1994	$7,500,000	$900,000	$1.20
1995	$10,312,500	$1,267,500	$1.69
1996	$12,000,000	$1,440,000	$1.92
1997	$18,750,000	$2,156,250	$2.88
1998	$21,375,000	$2,250,000	$3.00
1999	$23,250,000	$2,673,750	$3.57
2000	$27,375,000	$3,011,250	$4.02
2001	$31,875,000	$3,225,000	$4.30
2002	$34,125,000	$3,375,000	$4.50
2003	$38,625,000	$3,422,700	$4.56

She had also compiled some additional information that may have been relevant in estimating the firm's future cost of capital. According to her investment banker, a loyal telescope customer and part-time comet hunter from the Southwest, SCI could issue new bonds, at par, with a coupon rate of 6.75 percent. The firm's existing bonds had been issued with a coupon rate of 7.5 percent, and they had six years remaining until maturity. Although SCI had recently traded around $18.00 per share, several analysts were estimating that the stock should be trading closer to $22.75 per share within a few months. The investment banker also noted that other firms in the industry tried to operate with close to 45 percent of their capital (in market value terms) in debt, and the remainder made up of common equity. Because of their small size, optics companies were unlikely to be able to successfully issue preferred stock on a regular basis.

Tom Dillon contributed some figures that he and the board of directors had discussed in the past few weeks. A broad index of regional stocks had returned 15 percent in recent years, but that return had been closer to sixteen percent over the past several months. Although SCI was in the habit of paying approximately 32 percent of earnings as dividends each year, the board had asked that this be increased to 40 percent." This anticipated increase was part of the reason that SCI had been asked to talk to investors at the conference. In his notes on the subject, Dillon had written that the board favored a capital structure that was higher in debt, suggesting that 60 percent of total capital would be more in line with their expectations. He also stressed that every effort would be made, at the conference, to find out whether or not any of the institutional investors would be interested in purchasing preferred shares from a company such as SCI.

Finally, Ruby put together several pieces of information relating the firm's shares to the market and discovered that SCI's stock was approximately ten percent more volatile, on average, than either a national or regional basket of similar-sized stocks. In addition, she discovered that an index of U.S. Treasury bonds was currently yielding 5.10 percent.

As they went ahead with their "dog and pony show" for potential investors, the folks at SCI considered the future of the company and its products. SCI was popular with customers and amateur astronomers, to be sure, but they were hesitant to assume that this popularity would spill over into the company's capital market success. In addition, Ruby wondered how new investors would change the profile of the board of directors; it was currently made up of insiders and prominent amateur astronomers from around the country. Although the growth of the firm increased its prestige and ability to expand into new types of products, she was concerned that new investors would bring new worries.

REQUIRED:

1. Discuss the difference between the concepts of the historical weighted-average cost of capital and the marginal cost of capital. [Note: The "Scope City, Incorporated (A)" case asks about book value or historical costs of capital, but an understanding of that case is not necessary for answering any of these questions or reviewing the concepts involved.]

2. Explain how the marginal cost of capital can be relevant when considering new investment projects.

3. Explain how the marginal cost of capital should change for all firms in the marketplace when, for instance, all interest rates increase. How should it change when there is a general decline in stock prices?

4. Calculate the marginal (weighted-average) cost of capital for SCI. In addition, explain what is meant by the term "optimal capital structure."

5. Calculate SCI's book value (historical) cost of capital. If this number is different from your answer to 4, above, please explain how the difference occurred.

6. The case mentioned that the board of directors wanted to increase the amount of leverage in the company over and above what was expected in the industry. Does this sound reasonable? Why would shareholders seek to increase leverage in such a fashion?

7. SCI has been given the opportunity to purchase one of its smaller competitors (see Scope City, Incorporated (A) for more information). If the company plans to execute such a purchase with an exchange of shares, what considerations must be taken into account? In general terms, what possible impact could such a merger have on SCI and its ownership?

Case 17

PUREDELL DISTRIBUTION, INC.

INTRODUCTION

Puredell Distribution, Inc. (PDI) is considering an expansion in its current fleet of 39 trucks. The need for another type of truck has arisen, and the current fleet has been inadequate in recent months to handle the demand for shipping services from Puredell customers. The company is considering a purchase of ten container haulers and thirty containers. The advisability of this expansion depends upon the firm's cost of capital.

BACKGROUND

Puredell Distribution, Inc. was founded in 1948 as Tindell Trucking, a small trucking service with only one delivery truck, operating in Memphis, Tennessee. Mark Tindell, the proprietor, gradually expanded business and hauling capability until 1972. The company had grown to 8 trucks, and served business needs for local deliveries. In 1973, the company was combined with Puritan Delivery Service, owned by Roger Waithe, to form Puredell Trucking. As a result of the combination, the firm became a partnership with a total of 14 trucks, and expanded its territory to include northern Mississippi and eastern Arkansas.

The firm was incorporated in 1988. Mark and Roger were both in their seventies, and were wanting to assure that the firm would easily pass to their relatives. Stock shares were allotted based on an agreement between Mark and Roger. In 1994, Roger died and his son, Sean, took over his father's managerial duties. Sean proved his competence at running the firm, to the extent that Mark felt he could retire with confidence. Sean convinced Mark to move the company toward an initial public offering of stock, to allow for family members to liquidate their shares, if they wished. The firm's IPO occurred in 1996, amid a robust stock market hungry for newly issued stock. Mark died in 2001. Most of the family members liquidated their shares by 2003. Sean still owns about 30% of the shares, and is the largest single shareholder. He serves as CEO for the corporation.

THE NEED FOR CONTAINER DELIVERY

An increasing number of Puredell customers have expressed the need for deliveries to clients who do not have the inventory capacity to handle large loads. This presents a problem for Puredell, since all of Puredell's delivery trucks are Parcel Vans and Straight Trucks; basically a truck cab with an enclosed box on the back. With Puredell's current trucks, delivery involves unloading at the destination into a warehouse or other storage facility. Many of the clients served by Puredell customers do not have warehouse facilities. Instead, they receive shipments via containers or trailers, which can be left on site and unloaded by the client at their convenience. This has ruled out Puredell as the shipper, since Puredell does not have this type of delivery capability. Several of Puredell's customers have indicated that Puredell needs to offer this service, or they will be forced to seek a delivery company that *does* have the capability to offer it.

Puredell would benefit not only from additional business from existing customers, but also will have the opportunity to compete for business that would not be available to them without the expansion.

FINANCIAL INFORMATION

A cashflow analysis was done based on sales forecasts from Puredell's marketing manager and on cost estimates compiled by accounting. Based on these estimates, the project is expected to have an internal rate of return of 12.47%. The risk associated with the expansion is not appreciably different than that faced by the firm at present. The total cost of the new fleet and containers is $2,360,000.

Market information necessary for calculating Puredell's marginal cost of capital (MCC) was readily available. First, the company's current capital structure of 42% debt, 6% preferred equity and 52% common equity appeared to be consistent with optimality at the firm's marginal tax rate of 31%. The firm had deviated above and below the current proportions of debt and preferred equity, and the financing costs seemed to increase. Although the cost increases from the past may have been caused by other factors, Sean seemed to be convinced of the optimality of the current structure.

Central Banking Trust (CBT) had extended relatively cheap pre-approved credit at 8.5% for the expansion. The credit limit was $554,000. Puredell could issue bonds at 12% in the current market. Sean didn't see any reason the bond cost would increase beyond 12% for the expansion under consideration. Puredell had $128,000 in retained earnings it could tap before having to issue new shares of common stock. Preferred stock could be issued, as well.

Puredell's current dividend levels are $1.15 per share for common stock, expected to grow at an average of 5% for at least another decade, perhaps longer. The preferred stock pays a dividend of $1.37. Current share prices are $9.69 per common share and $11.50 per preferred share. Sam expects a $.70 per share issue cost for common stock and $.60 per share for preferred stock.

Sean decided to reinforce the analysis by considering two analysis methodologies to estimate the MCC in addition to the discounted cashflow model. Information was readily available to make use of the CAPM (capital asset pricing model) to estimate the cost of equity. The stock market's compound return, based on a widely diversified portfolio, was 14.8% for the past 15 years, and the firm's historical beta was 1.20. Average treasury yields were about 5.02% for treasury bonds.

The 'bond yield plus risk premium' approach was frequently used to come up with an alternative cost of common equity. Sean knew that the risk premium used with this model was subjectively determined, so he chose a risk premium he felt he could justify, 7%. Because Puredell had a relatively large flotation (or 'issue') cost, Sean was somewhat concerned that these last two alternative models did not differentiate between internal (retained earnings) and external (newly issued common stock) equity. Stockholders' usual insistence on plenty of analysis to back up the final verdict, though, convinced Sean to add the alternative methods to the analysis.

REQUIRED

1. Construct the marginal cost of capital schedule, for each of the alternative models for estimating the cost of equity. Use copies of the graph provided on the next page.

2. Plot the project (the expansion), overlaid with each of the three MCC schedules.

3. Evaluate the project with the exact cost of funding the $2.3 million under each MCC scenario.

4. Do the methods agree as to the accept reject criteria? If not, develop arguments for the use of each cost estimation method, and decide which one would be best for the decision.

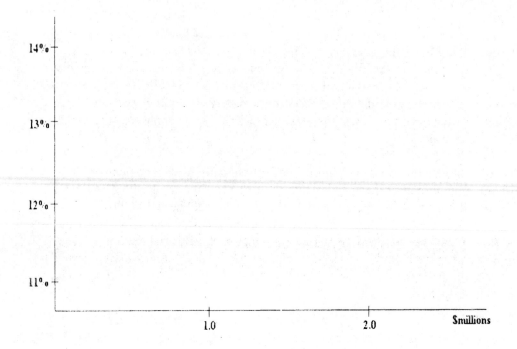

SECTION 7

WORKING CAPITAL MANAGEMENT

Case 18

NCI CORPORATION

Roger Simkin, general manager of Norfolk Cabinet, Inc. (NCI), sat in his office observing the last major shipment of kitchen and bathroom cabinets for the year being loaded into cargo containers. The containers would be loaded onto cargo ships headed for ports up and down the eastern seaboard and Gulf of Mexico, destined for retail outlets and contractors from Texas to Massachussetts. Unfortunately, the demand for these products was curiously seasonal. The slow season was beginning, from September to February. Roger faced the unpleasant task of reducing work schedules for the majority of his employees, and he knew from experience that some of them would simply be unable to make ends meet with so few hours to work. He really had no choice, though, since virtually no warehouse space was available on the waterfront, unless exhorbitant rents were paid!

Invariably, about a third of his plant laborers would seek other employment. A small positive aspect of this was that it made slightly more work for the workers who stayed, but it was far from an ideal situation. In the spring, Roger would face the reverse task of hiring workers for the high production period from March until the following August. Roger thought about how much he hated doing both tasks. He was seriously considering initiating a new proposal that Ed, his assistant manager, had suggested; of all things, producing caskets in the off season!

Roger had balked at the idea at first. It seemed a rather morbid thing to pursue. But as the end of the high production season had neared, he was seriously considering it. He had no idea who his customers would be. The ultimate consumer of the product could not be identified until, well, they were dead! Neither he nor Ed knew anything about marketing caskets. The idea, however, had merit; death and the demand for caskets probably wasn't seasonal, but if it were, wouldn't more people die in the winter?

The major benefit Roger saw was that his factory could operate year-round. This involved some major efficiencies in terms of hiring and training cost savings. Another advantage was that, according to Ed, the operating margin for caskets (that NCI already had the capability to produce) was about 40%, whereas their traditional product only had a 23%

operating margin (on average). In essence, the firm could operate year round with a new product offering that was even more profitable than cabinets.

THE CASKET INDUSTRY

It is often said that there are two things that one can always count on, death and taxes. For a long time it could be said that at least one of them was easy to perform. However, times have changed, and the industry of death has changed along with it. The days when one would just send their deceased loved one to the funeral home and leave everything to the funeral home are virtually over.

The reason for this shift can be traced to a phenomenon that has been sweeping across the United States. In an effort to cut the costs of funerals, consumers have started to look at the low cost alternative of buying the casket from a third party. This demand by consumers has led to an explosion of low cost casket outlets that offer quality caskets at wholesale prices. The concept is simple; you walk into your local casket outlet and look over the selections. Upon finding the ideal casket for your loved one, you would purchase the casket at the store and have it sent to the funeral home.

The popularity of this arrangement becomes obvious. The average funeral home marks up the price of a casket purchased from the manufacturer anywhere from three hundred to six hundred percent. The result is a $1200 casket that ends up being as much as $4000 by the time its lowered into the ground. Casket outlets are vastly cheaper because they apply a very small mark-up. The same $1200 casket may sell for just $1400 at a casket outlet. The reason that they can allow these small markups is twofold. First, they are not a funeral home, so the expenses incurred in the actual funeral process do not apply to them. Second, they sell so many caskets that they eventually reach economies of scale.

As discounters have increased in number, so have the number of casket manufacturers who are willing to sell their products to the general public. Regional manufacturers like the Catskill Casket Company and Casket Royale have begun selling the same caskets to the public as they sell to the funeral homes. The difference is that they sell them with just a ten to twenty percent markup. This has become a lucrative business for the casket manufactures with much of their profits now coming from either direct public sales or discounter sales.

Despite the benefit to consumers, funeral homes are fighting this movement tooth and nail. According to the Federal Trade Commission, up to forty percent of the average funeral price is the price of the casket. Funeral homes face a huge loss in profits if the discounters and casket manufacturers are allowed to gain a foot-hold in the industry. The stakes are especially high for the big funeral chains. Public corporations like Carriage Services, Incorporated stand to lose millions if casket prices drop even slightly.

GOVERNMENT INTERVENTION

Inevitably, funeral homes have tried to keep their advantage and hold on to their profits. In fact, they've been trying to keep their advantage for almost two decades. Up until 1984 funeral homes required customers to purchase caskets and coffins only from them. That rule was the main reason why there was no selling to the public. That changed when the Federal Trade Commission made the practice illegal (16 C.F.R. Part 453).

However, funeral homes found a way around the rule. If someone bought a casket from a discounter, the funeral home would charge a handling fee to move the casket from the discounter to the funeral home. The handling charge was often just as high, if not higher than their own markups. That practice suppressed the discounters, but it also got the attention of the Federal Trade Commission again. In 1994 the FTC made it illegal for funeral homes to charge any handling fee (16 C.F.R. Part 453 (1994)). This paved the way for dozens of casket discounters to enter the market.

Even after the ruling, funeral homes have apparently found another loophole. They now charge a much larger amount for overhead than they did before. When a casket is delivered to them from a discounter or manufacturer, they have been known to charge as much as two or three thousand dollars extra in overhead. That move has casket manufacturers and discounters crying 'foul!' It probably will only be a matter of time before the FTC gets involved yet again.

The whole situation has left the casket manufacturers in a precarious situation. The vast majority of their sales still occurs with funeral homes. Selling caskets to discounters or to the public would create a potentially lucrative source of sales, but would also strain their relationship with the funeral homes. Not selling to the discounters or the public would secure their relationship with the funeral homes, but might also lead to falling revenue if the discounters are able to use the basic rule of supply and demand to drive down casket prices.

A SAMPLE COMPANY

One example of the casket makers' dilemma is the case of the Catskill Casket Company. Seeing the shift in focus throughout the industry, Catskill attempted to start selling caskets to discounters and the public while continuing their accounts with the funeral homes. The result was the cancellation of their funeral home accounts. The casket maker also claimed that the funeral homes bullied Catskill's suppliers into not selling to Catskill anymore. While Catskill still does sell to the public, their relationship with funeral homes has changed from confederate to competitor. Boycotts from funeral homes are becoming more and more common as discounters cut into funeral home revenue. Catskill ended up writing a letter to the Federal Trade Commission complaining about the practices that had been used by the funeral homes. Apparently, some funeral homes have managed to not only bully the casket makers into not selling caskets to the public, but the have also convinced vault and tomb manufacturers to not sell their products to any casket manufacturer that does sell to the public. Up until this case the FTC still had not taken any action against the funeral homes that Catskill claims tried to intimidate them.

So far, Catskill is considered an extreme example. However, as more casket manufacturers sell to the public, the funeral homes may become more aggressive with their tactics. Funeral homes are already in the process of using legal tools to stop the proliferation of discounters. In many cases this includes lawsuits and/or massive lobbying campaigns to keep archaic funeral laws on the books.

LEGAL ISSUES

In some states it is actually illegal for casket makers to sell their products to anyone else except to funeral homes. Discounters in Georgia have been under threat of being shut down for months now because of the funeral laws currently on the books in that state. Right now there are seven states that have laws against selling caskets other than to funeral homes. Most of the states are in the southeast (Alabama, Georgia, South Carolina) where funeral homes are keeping a death grip on the market.

The Funeral Home Directors Association has been fighting along with the large chain funeral homes to keep those laws on the books. They insist that only a trained mortician should handle a casket and that there is a loss of quality when using outside casket vendors. However, despite what they may insist, consumers are starting to wake up to the realization that the exact same casket selling for $4,300 at the funeral home is being sold for $1,200 by the discounter and $1,000 by the casket manufacturer.

There is even a small fringe of the industry that is now pushing the idea of homemade caskets as the ultimate low cost alternative. A company known as Homemade Casket Plans sells not the casket itself, but the plans to make one. For $19.95 you will receive eight pages of detailed plans showing you how to make you very own casket. The company estimates that it will cost about $300 on the wood for a basic casket and a little more for a fancy one. They even claim that you can modify it into a viable piece of furniture until it is needed.

If making one's own casket sounds like too much work then how about renting one? Massachusetts has actually passed legislation protecting someone's right to use rented caskets for funerals. The idea is that you rent an expensive looking casket for the wake and funeral, then buy a less expensive casket for the actual burial or cremation. While it may make some people squeamish, it is a potential low cost alternative to the standard funeral.

The funeral homes insist that their markups are warranted because they are offering more than the discounters are. They cite their embalming costs and other costs involved in properly getting the body ready for the funeral. They also claim the discounters and direct manufactures simply don't give the personal touch that most funeral homes do. They also defend the laws against non-funeral homes still insisting that trained professional morticians should be the ones that deal with the casket.

With a rash of recent mergers, the funeral homes have a distinct advantage over the discounters in terms of resources. The two largest funeral home corporations have resources that dwarf those of the average casket manufacturer or discounter. The mergers have come about partly because of the discounters and partly because of slowing of business. In virtually every state there are more funeral homes than are actually needed. To gain an advantage in an already saturated market, funeral homes have merged with corporate funeral home operators. They hope that their new parent company can give them the resource advantage that they need.

Some casket makers have already made the choice of which side they are on. The largest casket manufacture, Batesville (a subsidiary of the Hillenbrand Corporation) held steadfast to the idea of only selling to funeral homes. Other, smaller casket manufacturers have followed suit and kept their relationship with the funeral homes. However, that approach does not do much for shareholder interests. The discounters represent a high growth, potentially lucrative market.

PRELIMINARY EXPECTATIONS

Roger had read about the detailed situation in the industry, and was skeptical about the ability of his current sales force, accustomed to dealing with home improvement chains and contractors, to find and nurture relationships with casket retailers. He was even less confident about selling directly to the public. He assumed that any sales to funeral homes were probably done through long-standing relationships between the homes and suppliers. The key, he thought, was to either contract with other manufacturers to make caskets for them, thus increasing their market share, or to hire some salespeople accustomed to developing relationships with casket retailers, where the caskets could be sold. He decided that if he was going to make the attempt, that it would be good to attempt both strategies.

To produce the average casket, Roger estimated total operating costs of about $700, and an average selling price directly to consumers of $1,100 and to retailers, a price of $980. Roger knew that there were some crucial questions that would have to be resolved before a decision could be made.

REQUIRED

1. What are the 'key risks' associated with NCI's entry into casket manufacturing/selling?

2. Is there a possibility that the firm's sales will increase throughout the year? Will NCI benefit from not having to rehire/retrain workers? Estimate of the benefit for both.

3. What is the operating margin for manufacturing caskets, assuming Roger's cost and price estimates are valid? How does the margin change as the target purchaser changes (i.e. direct, to retailers, to wholesalers. to other manufacturers, etc.)?

4. Estimate the proportion (and number per year) of caskets you would expect to sell to each market mentioned in number 3. Justify your estimate with some logical argument.

5. Forecast an income statement for the next year, assuming NCI *does* begin producing caskets this season (in the slow months).

6. Based on your forecast, should NCI proceed with the manufacture of caskets? Or should Roger gear down for the slow season, as usual?

Exhibit 1. Monthly Income Statements

	JAN	FEB	MAR	APR	MAY	JUN
Sales	$151,291	$189,003	$359,387	$1,823,265	$2,108,336	$1,984,760
Cost of Goods Sold	34,803	47,770	90,014	459,960	510,040	499,993
Other Variable Costs	39,751	56,231	102,323	648,725	598,296	510,035
Fixed Operating Costs	60,106	59,960	61,033	60,013	60,986	65,270
Operating Profit	16,632	25,042	106,018	654,566	939,014	909,462
Interest Expenses	22,434	22,337	22,239	22,140	22,040	21,939
Earnings Before Taxes	(5,802)	2,705	83,779	632,426	916,974	887,523
Income Taxes	(1,625)	757	23,458	177,079	256,753	248,507
Net Income	($4,178)	$1,948	$60,321	$455,347	$660,221	$639,017

	JUL	AUG	SEP	OCT	NOV	DEC
Sales	$2,018,365	$1,750,059	$299,444	$69,380	$287,433	$129,81
Cost of Goods	430,579	460,980	92,367	12,885	78,820	31,067
Other Variable	528,366	482,987	59,881	29,903	69,704	32,001
Fixed Operating Costs	62,990	68,529	62,100	60,100	59,112	61,024
Operating Profit	996,430	737,563	85,096	(33,508)	79,797	5,720
Interest Expenses	21,837	21,734	21,630	21,525	21,419	21,312
Earnings Before Taxes	974,593	715,829	63,466	(55,033)	58,378	(15,592)
Income Taxes	272,886	200,432	17,770	(15,409)	16,346	(4,366)
Net Income	$701,707	$515,397	$45,695	($39,624)	$42,032	($11,226)

	TOTAL 1998
Sales	$11,170,534
Cost of Goods Sold	2,749,277
Other Variable Costs	3,158,202
Fixed Operating Costs	741,221
Operating Profit	4,521,833
Interest Expenses	262,585
Earnings Before Taxes	4,259,247
Income Taxes	1,192,589
Net Income	$3,066,658

REFERENCES

Cabell, B. (1998). Retail Casket Sellers Feel Boxed In@. *CNN Online*: www.cnn.com

Consumer Casket USA: www.consumercasket.com

Fairclough, G. (1997). Casket Stores Offer Bargins to Die For. *Wall Street Journal* February 19, B1/C1-B2/C1.

Federal Trade Commission. Part 453 - Funeral Industry Practices Revised Rule. www.ftc.gov/bcp/conline/pubs/buspubs/funeral/rule.htm

Funeral and Memorial Services of America (FAMSA) www.vbiweb.champlain.edu/famsa/index.htm

Homemade Casket Plans of America: www.volcano.net/~johnstone/caskhome.html

Horn, M. (1998). The Deathcare Business. *US News and World Report*, March 23, 43-48.

Otani, E. (1998). Not-So-Grim Reapers. *Los Angeles Times Online:* www.latimes.com

The authors wish to express their thanks to Hampton University's Honors College for their support of the gathering of background information for this case.

Case 19

MCGHEE CORPORATION

For as long as he could remember, Calvin McGhee had enjoyed long car trips. As a child he had spent summers travelling with his family, by car, to most parts of the United States. To him, road trips were the most fun one could have, especially if you could stop along the way and enjoy the sights.

Not surprisingly, Calvin became a long-haul trucker after college. It paid good wages and had the advantage of allowing him to see the country from the cab of his truck. He couldn't do any sightseeing this way, of course, but he figured that there was always time for that later.

Six years of open road trucking took its toll, however, and Calvin was tired of the long hours and poor working conditions. As he became more and more discontent with the trucking industry, he started to look for ways to use his knowledge to start a business of his own. Calvin founded McGhee Corporation in the late 1980s.

McGhee specialized in "jobber" sales at truck stops and travel centers across the U.S. and Canada. "Rack jobbers" came in and stocked one part of the store, maintaining inventory and keeping track of consumer interests and popular products. In many cases, these items were the only shopping opportunity that truckers had during the week. Calvin had been able to start small by capitalizing on his knowledge of the trucker lifestyle and the needs of those on the road. Initially, he contracted for shelf space at truck stops in his region and filled that space with wholesale goods he found at closeout sales and business auctions. Truckers had responded by snapping up the toys, books and small appliances that Calvin thought would be appreciated. Within two years Calvin had hired a dozen other employees to help with his routes, and after another two years he needed dozens more. In addition, he had found ways to buy imported goods and keep his inventory consistent across the country.

GET YOUR MOTOR RUNNING

By the end of 2003, McGhee Corporation had become one of the largest jobbers in the U.S. The firm sponsored many products for import, with its own brand names, and had successfully offered Internet ordering only a year before. The company sold everything from video games and textbooks to laptop computers online and maintained job racks and gift sections in thousands of locations across the country. Finally, Calvin McGhee thought he would be able to take the time to travel and be a tourist again.

In order for Calvin to do this, however, it was necessary for him to spend less and less time in the office. To this end, he had spent time the previous year hiring and training a new assistant and teaching her the intricacies of the rack jobber business. Sheryl Plath was just a few months out of school and trying as hard as she could to learn everything about McGhee and his business. Mr. McGhee had placed a great deal of faith in her, and it was obvious that he planned to put at least part of the future of his company in her hands.

THE CASH-TO-CASH CYCLE

Calvin had challenged Ms. Plath using a series of exercises involving the firm's accounting numbers. This week, the lesson was in the area of "working capital management." In addition to her regular tasks, Sheryl was expected to work on this problem and present her findings to Mr. McGhee at the end of the week. Calvin had prepared a balance sheet (Exhibit 1) and some additional information about the firm's cost structure (Exhibit 2). Both statements were based upon 365 days in the firm's fiscal year.

Exhibit 1. McGhee Corporation. Balance Sheet, December 31, 2003.

Cash	$140,000
Accounts receivable	$1,225,000
Inventory	$875,000
Current assets	$2,240,000
Net fixed assets	$2,135,000
Total assets	$4,375,000
Accounts payable	$700,000
Accruals	$140,000
Notes payable - bank	$788,000
Current maturities of LT Debt	$87,500
Current liabilities	$1,715,000
Long-term debt	$962,500
Common stock & PIC	$297,000
Retained earnings	$1,400,000
Total liabilities & equity	$4,375,000

Exhibit 2. Selected Income Statement Information, December 31, 2003.

Sales Revenue, net	$15,968,750
Cost of Goods Sold, net	$10,675,000
Purchases, net	$11,252,500
Operating expenses	$4,462,500

The current lesson was about the firm's "cash-to-cash" cycles. Calvin stressed that working through the difference between the cash-to-cash cycle for assets and the cycle for liabilities could help Sheryl understand the need for short-term borrowing. "We can only get so much credit from our suppliers," he reminded her. He gave her an outline of the process and its importance (Exhibit 3).

As he left for another road trip, Calvin smiled and reminded Sheryl that "every minute you spend with this finance stuff now is twenty minutes saved later on." He would be back on Friday afternoon, and they could talk about the firm's working capital then.

Exhibit 3. Memo Regarding Firm's Cash Cycle: 12/31/03.

Sheryl:

The usual thing to worry about is the difference between assets and liabilities. If assets convert to cash faster than liabilities, that's a good thing, but that's a very unusual situation. More often, your liabilities will be "due," essentially, before your receivables have come in fully. Cash sales, when they actually happen, will help shorten the asset cash-to-cash cycle and make your job easier -- we rarely have significant cash sales, as you've probably learned in the past few months.

To figure out how the assets and liabilities work together on this, you'll need to have some numbers in front of you. In particular, you'll want to know what our average daily sales and cost of goods sold are, and what our average purchases are. Finally, it would be useful to know our average daily operating expenses, too.

Once you have all of that stuff, convert the balance sheet into its daily equivalent. For example: part of the asset cash-to-cash cycle is the daily level of cash on hand. You can find this by dividing the cash amount on the balance sheet by the average daily sales figure to get "days cash." Accounts receivable is also directly related to our sales figures, but when looking at average inventory be sure to consider our daily COGS instead. On the other side of the balance sheet, payables are closely related to average daily purchases and accruals are related to operating expenses.

The asset cash-to-cash cycle is the combination of the "days cash," the similar measure for accounts receivable, and the inventory "days". This is roughly how long it takes us to convert a sale into cash, on average. For the liabilities, we look at "days payable" and "days accruals" as mentioned. These two numbers tell us how much we rely upon suppliers and employees for credit, and added together give us the number of days in the liability cash-to-cash cycle.

The difference between the total days in the asset cycle and the total days in the liability cycle is the number of days' worth of financing we'll need during the period. When used with our daily COGS number, it can tell us how much bank financing we might need during that time. If nothing else, it provides a rough estimate for using when we plan for a new year, and it helps us evaluate the rest of our working capital.

REQUIRED

1. Using the information in Exhibits 1 and 2, calculate McGhee's average daily sales, average daily cost of goods sold, average daily purchases, and average operating expenses. How much control does the firm have over each of these items?

2. Convert the asset portion of the firm's balance sheet in Exhibit 1 into its daily equivalent. How many days does the firm have in its asset "cash-to-cash" cycle?

3. Convert the short-term liabilities on the balance sheet into their daily equivalents. How many days are in McGhee's liability "cash-to-cash" cycle?

4. Using your answers from 2 and 3, above, determine the number of days that the firm may need to finance itself during the cash-to-cash cycle. How can this number be used to determine the amount of external financing necessary?

5. What types of external funding sources are appropriate for supporting a working capital deficit of the type that is described in Mr. McGhee's memo? Why are some sources more appropriate than others?

6. What are some ways that McGhee could make the asset cash-to-cash cycle shorter?

7. What are some ways that McGhee could make the liability cash-to-cash cycle longer?

8. What considerations would need to be made when changing the company's terms on receivables, and changing policies on other current assets or liabilities? What complications and/or difficulties has Mr. McGhee left out of his memo?

SECTION 8

RISK AND RETURN

CASE 20

LABELTECH CORPORATION

INTRODUCTION

Labeltech Corporation is a manufacturer of adhesive labels for business and consumer markets. The firm makes label sheets for laser and inkjet printers for sale through retail stores, and custom prints labels, envelopes, and other business products for direct sale through mail order. The firm has been a publicly traded company for eighteen years.

STEVE SUSWAL, NEW GUY

Steve Suswal was recently hired by Labeltech Corporation as their new associate financial manager. He works under the Vice President for Finance, Roger Franklin. Steve was in his third week of work for Labeltech, and had mastered the repetitive operational tasks to which he had been assigned. It was not quite what Steve had expected; he had just graduated from an MBA program, and felt that he had much more to contribute to the company's welfare than just operational tasks.

Steve began examining the financial condition and performance of the firm on his own time. He had done a complete ratio analysis, and had calculated the degree of operating and financial leverage, and had found the firm to be rather conservative in its approach to debt financing. Steve had particularly enjoyed learning the theories of leverage and capital structure, and the tie-in to the risk of the firm. On his own, he had come up with the idea that if a firm was well below their optimal debt level, that an increase in value should consistently follow increases in debt levels, and vice versa.

Steve was also no stranger to the political environment in a company, and wanted to let Roger know what he was up to. Steve also wanted Roger to know that he was going the extra mile in analyzing the firm's financial leverage with hopes of coming up with some useful changes that could be recommended. He decided to talk with Roger on Monday morning, which seemed like a good time. The stresses of the work week were not upon them yet, and Roger usually showed up at least an hour before everyone else.

MONDAY MORNING

Steve arrived about two hours early on Monday morning. He had prepared some materials for Roger to look at, and had rehearsed what he wanted to say in a well- structured way. When Roger arrived, Steve waited about fifteen minutes and then knocked on Roger's door.

"Come on in, Steve. Have a cup of coffee," Roger said.

"Thanks. I don't mind if I do," Steve replied. Steve didn't even have to wait for an opportunity:

"So, are you acclimating to the company yet?" Roger asked.

"Oh, yes," Steve replied. "I am actually enjoying the position a lot. I've even been working on a little analysis on my own time. Have you ever analyzed the company's use of debt and its effect on cost of capital?" Steve asked.

"Well, that depends on what you mean by analyze. In the past, we've just used book values of debt and equity to come up with a debt ratio. Ours is right there with the average for our industry, so we just kind of assume that it is close to optimal," Roger said. "You have a lot of data available, if you want to try and determine an optimal level, though."

Steve was surprised that Roger was so accepting of an assumption of optimality of the industry average. Roger had even more of an academic background in finance theory than Steve did. Roger had even completed coursework toward a doctoral degree several years prior, but had not continued because of the lucrative position Labeltech had offered him. Steve was surprised that Roger would just say "Go for it" so quickly.

"I'd be happy to work on that," Steve said. "I already have an idea about the approach."

"Good!" Roger said. "I'll look forward to seeing what you come up with." Roger smiled a smile that seemed strangely large. "Well, I have a conference call in five minutes. We'd better get to work."

"I have a full day, too," Steve replied. "I'll let you know what I come up with."

HISTORICAL DATA

Steve was able to get historical balance sheets for the past eighteen years, which he used to compute debt ratios. He wasn't very concerned about the industry norm, since there was no indication that the industry norm was an optimal debt level. He also was not so concerned about market values of debt and equity, since market values were not totally under the control of the firm. He wanted to see if he could identify which book value debt ratio resulted in the best value for the firm.

Steve saw that the stock price had trended upward over time, and wondered if the actual stock price was what he really needed to look at. He decided that the deviation away from the trend line was more appropriate. He ran a regression to output predicted values as a trendline. The regression errors thus represented the deviation away from the fitted regression line. Steve created a table with the stock value, the predicted values (trendline), regression errors (deviation from trend), and the debt to assets ratio, by quarter. The resulting table is Exhibit 3.

Steve ran a correlation analysis to see if higher debt ratios were correlated with larger positive deviations of the stock price from the trend, and lower debt ratios were correlated with larger negative deviations from the trend. The results of the regression are presented in Exhibit 1.

Exhibit 1. Correlation Output: Debt ratio versus Price Deviation from Trend.

	D/A	Deviation*
D/A	1	
Deviation*	0.302888	1

* price deviation from fitted trend line

Exhibit 2. Plot of Debt Ratio versus Price Deviation from Trend.

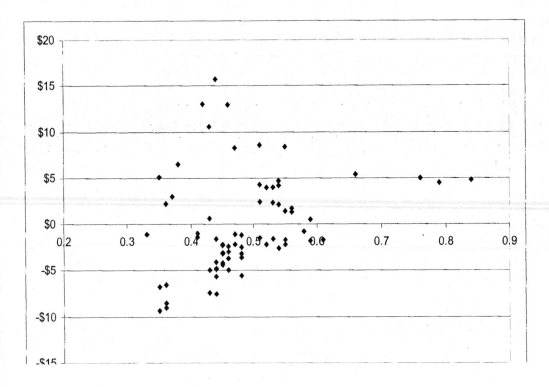

REQUIRED

1. Based on Steve's correlation and data plot, what would you conclude about the relationship between the debt ratio and the price deviation from trend over time?

2. Evaluate Steve's methodology. Be sure to consider the optimal debt ratio model and its assumptions.

3. How practical is it for a firm to identify its optimal debt ratio?

4. What should a future business practitioner conclude concerning the concept of an optimal debt ratio?

Exhibit 3. Debt and Stock Value Data.

Trend	Quarter	Stock Value	Trendline	Deviation*	D/A
1	**1986(2)**	$16.12	11.1361074	4.9838926	0.76
2	**1986(3)**	$16.12	11.5906204	4.5293796	0.79
3	**1986(4)**	$16.87	12.0451333	4.8248667	0.84
4	**1987(1)**	$17.87	12.4996463	5.3703537	0.66
5	**1987(2)**	$17.12	12.9541593	4.1658407	0.54
6	**1987(3)**	$17.37	13.4086723	3.9613277	0.53
7	**1987(4)**	$18.12	13.8631853	4.2568147	0.51
8	**1988(1)**	$19.00	14.3176983	4.6823017	0.54
9	**1988(2)**	$18.75	14.7722113	3.9777887	0.52
10	**1988(3)**	$17.50	15.2267243	2.2732757	0.53
11	**1988(4)**	$18.12	15.6812373	2.4387627	0.51
12	**1989(1)**	$18.25	16.1357503	2.1142497	0.54
13	**1989(2)**	$18.87	16.5902633	2.2797367	0.53
14	**1989(3)**	$18.75	17.0447762	1.7052238	0.56
15	**1989(4)**	$18.87	17.4992892	1.3707108	0.55
16	**1990(1)**	$19.25	17.9538022	1.2961978	0.56
17	**1990(2)**	$18.87	18.4083152	0.4616848	0.59
18	**1990(3)**	$18.12	18.8628282	-0.7428282	0.58
19	**1990(4)**	$17.50	19.3173412	-1.8173412	0.59
20	**1991(1)**	$18.12	19.7718542	-1.6518542	0.61
21	**1991(2)**	$19.00	20.2263672	-1.2263672	0.48
22	**1991(3)**	$19.25	20.6808802	-1.4308802	0.51
23	**1991(4)**	$19.50	21.1353932	-1.6353932	0.55
24	**1992(1)**	$20.00	21.5899062	-1.5899062	0.53
25	**1992(2)**	$19.87	22.0444191	-2.1744191	0.52
26	**1992(3)**	$20.37	22.4989321	-2.1289321	0.47
27	**1992(4)**	$19.25	22.9534451	-3.7034451	0.46
28	**1993(1)**	$19.25	23.4079581	-4.1579581	0.45
29	**1993(2)**	$18.87	23.8624711	-4.9924711	0.46
30	**1993(3)**	$21.12	24.3169841	-3.1969841	0.45
31	**1993(4)**	$22.50	24.7714971	-2.2714971	0.45
32	**1994(1)**	$22.75	25.2260101	-2.4760101	0.48
33	**1994(2)**	$22.50	25.6805231	-3.1805231	0.48
34	**1994(3)**	$23.75	26.1350361	-2.3850361	0.46
35	**1994(4)**	$24.37	26.5895491	-2.2195491	0.45

Trend	Quarter	Stock Value	Trendline	Deviation*	D/A
37	1995(2)	$26.12	27.4985750	-1.3785750	0.41
38	1995(3)	$20.50	27.9530880	-7.4530880	0.43
39	1995(4)	$23.50	28.4076010	-4.9076010	0.44
40	1996(1)	$25.87	28.8621140	-2.9921140	0.46
41	1996(2)	$25.25	29.3166270	-4.0666270	0.44
42	1996(3)	$26.75	29.7711400	-3.0211400	0.45
43	1996(4)	$25.50	30.2256530	-4.7256530	0.44
44	1997(1)	$25.12	30.6801660	-5.5601660	0.48
45	1997(2)	$25.50	31.1346790	-5.6346790	0.44
46	1997(3)	$26.67	31.5891920	-4.9191920	0.43
47	1997(4)	$24.50	32.0437050	-7.5437050	0.44
48	1998(1)	$28.12	32.4982179	-4.3782179	0.45
49	1998(2)	$29.37	32.9527309	-3.5827309	0.48
50	1998(3)	$30.87	33.4072439	-2.5372439	0.54
51	1998(4)	$31.67	33.8617569	-2.1917569	0.55
52	1999(1)	$33.25	34.3162699	-1.0662699	0.47
53	1999(2)	$35.37	34.7707829	0.5992171	0.43
54	1999(3)	$34.25	35.2252959	-0.9752959	0.41
55	1999(4)	$38.67	35.6798089	2.9901911	0.37
56	2000(1)	$41.25	36.1343219	5.1156781	0.35
57	2000(2)	$38.75	36.5888349	2.1611651	0.36
58	2000(3)	$30.50	37.0433479	-6.5433479	0.36
59	2000(4)	$28.12	37.4978608	-9.3778608	0.35
60	2001(1)	$29.37	37.9523738	-8.5823738	0.36
61	2001(2)	$29.37	38.4068868	-9.0368868	0.36
62	2001(3)	$32.12	38.8613998	-6.7413998	0.35
63	2001(4)	$38.25	39.3159128	-1.0659128	0.33
64	2002(1)	$46.25	39.7704258	6.4795742	0.38
65	2002(2)	$48.55	40.2249388	8.3250612	0.55
66	2002(3)	$49.24	40.6794518	8.5605482	0.51
67	2002(4)	$49.36	41.1339648	8.2260352	0.47
68	2003(1)	$52.14	41.5884778	10.5515222	0.43
69	2003(2)	$54.94	42.0429908	12.8970092	0.46
70	2003(3)	$58.20	42.4975038	15.7024962	0.44
71	2003(4)	$56.02	42.9520167	13.0679833	0.42

Case 21

ROTH FINANCIAL ADVISORS

Steve Johnson had worked very hard in college to prepare himself for being a financial advisor. The tough classes and long hours had paid off so far, and he was finding enough challenges and wrinkles in this job to keep him focused and interested. His latest task involved educating investors and small business owners about their financial alternatives and the basics of investments and portfolio theory.

Roth Financial Advisors (RFA) served a diverse set of clients, some of whom were quite sophisticated, financially, and others who were just starting to invest. The company had been founded almost ten years ago after Hugo Roth and his college roommate had set up shop in a two-room storefront. The roommate had soon decided that the financial services industry was not tangible enough for his tastes, but Hugo Roth had found plenty of bright young minds to come aboard in the meantime. As the firm grew, Roth developed a reputation for training his associates and helping them establish themselves in the business. Hugo Roth's personal reputation for honesty and fair dealing benefited the firm's reputation, and RFA had built a large customer base during its short life.

THE NEW GUY

Steve Johnson had become used to the long hours at work and the extra reading and "assignments" that Roth constantly asked him to work on. He realized that he still had a lot to learn about financial services, and finance in general, and he looked forward to each assignment.

Recently Roth had asked Steve to develop a presentation and a set of educational materials regarding the different types of risks that investors might face when placing their money with the firm. Some of the information that they had collected for this assignment was rather rudimentary, but the difficulty of the task came in explaining things clearly to investors.

147

Steve's assignment had come about when one of Roth's longtime associates had relayed a question from a client: what is this whole risk thing, anyway? There was no simple way to answer this question, unfortunately, but Hugo Roth had asked Steve to break it down into its simplest components and figure out a way to show clients how risk was treated in the financial markets and when making investment decisions. The presentation could be as basic or as complex as Steve felt was necessary.

According to Roth, there were two ways to understand risk: risk could be measured in conjunction with an investor's portfolio, or risk could be measured, in a traditional sense, as the chance of loss on some project or single investment. He had stressed that Steve would have to work out these two different meanings of risk in the presentation and make sense of each. In addition, Roth was concerned that the techniques used in finance appeared to be complicated and tedious, and he wanted this presentation to point out an example of each concept discussed and demonstrate how the techniques actually made sense when considered carefully. It was Roth's belief that even the most sophisticated clients could benefit from a good example now and then.

BY THE NUMBERS

Roth provided several sets of numbers for Steve to use in the presentation. The first set was a group of returns for three different stocks, classified by the type of economy that these stocks might face in the future and the return each was likely to experience in the different situations (Exhibit 1). To be conservative, each future scenario was considered to be equally likely. Roth was convinced that there was some way to measure and compare the risks of these three potential investments, together and as separate purchases, but he suggested that Steve might have to be creative when coming up with such a measure.

In addition to measures of risk for individual stocks and/or projects, Roth wanted the presentation to deal with how investors measured risk when a portfolio was being considered. Roth pulled some representative numbers from the Internet: annualized quarterly returns for a market index and two different stocks (Exhibit 2). He indicated to Steve that the proper measure of risk for a portfolio would have to be calculated using this kind of data series.

Exhibit 1. Probable returns for several different investments.

Economic Situation	Waxell Inc.	Stewart Inc.	Edelman Inc.
recession	-2.00%	2.54%	15.46%
no change	6.57%	4.35%	7.50%
growth	9.21%	6.78%	4.60%
boom	14.50%	9.71%	1.54%

Historical Correlations:

Waxell & Stewart	0.357
Stewart & Edelman	-0.275
Waxell & Edelman	-0.071

Exhibit 2. Annualized Monthly Returns: Market Index and Two Traded Stocks.

Quarter	Market Index	Stock A	Stock B
1	5.08%	2.37%	1.05%
2	5.08%	1.37%	11.90%
3	5.50%	1.30%	-1.50%
4	1.19%	7.71%	-7.37%
5	-1.79%	1.14%	13.26%
6	-1.62%	1.51%	-0.70%
7	-1.13%	6.29%	6.42%
8	5.09%	3.88%	9.87%
9	8.10%	8.26%	-0.47%
10	0.84%	0.61%	-3.17%
11	1.70%	0.12%	5.12%
12	2.74%	0.90%	-15.58%
13	6.03%	10.83%	18.81%
14	5.71%	10.31%	9.84%
15	8.64%	35.37%	-2.12%
16	11.00%	22.64%	-10.67%
17	0.49%	7.31%	-7.72%
18	7.90%	2.22%	-17.83%
19	7.25%	10.51%	-1.84%
20	0.88%	3.76%	3.44%
21	6.17%	19.47%	-1.31%
22	3.67%	5.99%	2.23%
23	2.08%	8.93%	7.42%
24	1.56%	10.81%	2.10%

After the office closed for the day and the phones stopped ringing, Steve felt that he could finally settle down and work on his risk material. He started a new pot of coffee and claimed the table in the nearby conference room to spread out his work. It would probably be a long night.

REQUIRED

1. Discuss the concept of stand-alone or project risk, and distinguish this risk, and its measures, from portfolio risk.

2. Using the information given in Exhibit 1, determine the most likely rate of return for each investment in the upcoming period. In addition, find the standard deviation of return for each investment.

3. Using your answer to 2, above, and assuming that investors can only invest in one of the three alternatives in Exhibit 1, use expected return and standard deviation to determine which alternative would be the most appropriate for a risk-averse investor. Justify your method of comparison.

4. Determine the expected return and standard deviation of a portfolio comprised of Waxell shares and Stewart shares in equal dollar amounts. Without making any calculations, explain how the computation would be more complex if you were to consider risk and return for a portfolio of Waxell, Stewart and Edelman shares.

5. Use the numbers in Exhibit 2 to determine the systematic risk (beta) of Stock A and Stock B. Which measure, beta or standard deviation, is more useful when analyzing stocks that are to be placed in a portfolio?

6. Referring to your solutions to the questions above, discuss how beta and standard deviation (volatility) are different. In addition, explain how systematic risk and unsystematic risk are different and how each risk is dealt with in the capital markets.

7. The Capital Asset Pricing Model (CAPM) relies upon beta as a measure of a firm's risk. Explain how the CAPM uses beta and illustrate, with an example, how the CAPM or the Security Market Line (SML) can be used to measure a firm's risk premium and required rate of return.

Case 22

SOUND ADVICE

INTRODUCTION

A recent graduate, Will Stevens, finds that his limited business experience may be enough to make him a "finance guru" at a small manufacturing firm. The manager and owner of this firm, a wizened acoustical engineer, uses the opportunity of reviewing the annual capital budget to ask some questions about his personal portfolio and the investments of his senior employees and shareholders. In addition, Will's parents have placed a great deal of faith in him and have asked questions about their portfolios and what choices they should make. In reconciling all of these different questions about risk and return, Will gains some useful insights into the value of some of the concepts he studied in college.

SOUND PRODUCTS, INC.

Will Stevens glanced at his "To Do" list again and wondered what priorities he should assign to each task. "They're *all* urgent," he thought, as he looked at the stack of papers which had accumulated during the past several weeks. Will had landed a great job right out of school, and he found working life to be altogether rewarding. His boss was Mike Jenner, owner and general manager of Sound Products, Incorporated. Sound Products manufactured and distributed audio equipment which was designed to please the type of consumers known as "stereophiles." Mike had started the company twenty years before, in his garage, and it had grown into one of the best known boutique firms in the industry. Since taking the job as Sound Product's business manager, Will had learned more about the stereo components business than he had ever wanted to know.

From what he had learned about Sound Products, though, Will recognized that Mike's expertise in business did not match his knowledge of acoustical engineering. Sound Products had benefited from a great deal of luck to achieve its market position, and Will saw many things that the firm could do differently. Being a new guy was challenging enough, but the role of business guru that Mike had attributed to him was becoming quite demanding. Will had spent endless nights reading everything he could get his hands on regarding business finance and operations management, hoping to stay ahead of Mike expectations and questions. Preparing for his role as business chieftain had also helped Will in his tasks outside of the office.

As the first person in his family to go to business school, Will was constantly bombarded from home with questions about personal finance. His mother was a biochemist with a great deal of business responsibility and respect within her firm; it had taken her nearly twenty years to rise to that position. His father had started out as an aeronautical engineer at NASA, ending up as a manager of one of the agency's regional research facilities. Around the Sunday afternoon dinner table, his mom and dad would quiz him about their retirement options and investment alternatives. He had tried to direct them to his favorite books on the subject, but that only increased the intensity and frequency of their questions. Coming up with answers to their questions was just another item on his list of things to get done.

WILL STEVENS, FINANCIAL GENIOUS

It was time for the Monday afternoon business meeting, which followed the usual Monday morning production meeting. Mike strolled into Will's tiny office and plopped down on the chair across from the desk. "What's the wise word today, O Anointed One?" Mike was pulling his chain, but Will knew that this meant there were big questions rattling around in the engineer's mind.

Will opened the discussion, while he still had the chance. "Mike, I've been looking at the list of things that you'd like to do for next year, and I've decided that I don't know enough about stereo equipment yet. And I figured that you could tell me about each project faster than you could write it down and let me read it." Will sat back and waited for Mike to take the stage.

"We've got a handle on the revenue and cost numbers, in general, for all three projects; those are in front of you. The first one involves introducing a new turntable that I've been working on for a couple of years. I'm not in love with it, mind you, but I think that it might be something our customers would want. We could probably sell a thousand units by the end of next year, and once it was out, word would spread to give us another thousand units each year after that. Plus, I want to give some as Christmas gifts." Mike grinned. "I think my daughter's still using her old department store record player just to spite me."

"Next," Mike continued, "we could go ahead with the line of automotive speakers that we discussed last week. That's the second proposal. I went over the numbers again with the guys on the floor and we think it could fly. With the popularity of luxury automobiles, and the availability of installation by professionals, we might be able to charge our customary markups. Of course, we haven't competed in the market for automotive audio since I wanted to bring out that combination 8-track/cassette deck in the late seventies. Who knew that 8-tracks were on their way out? Unlike that project, this one is probably a winner.

"Finally, the shop wanted me to reconsider a line of noise-canceling speakers for home audio. We hold the patents on the necessary electronics, and we think there would be a considerable demand for such a thing down the road, especially among folks who live in urban areas where there is a great deal of ambient noise. A couple thousands units per year, to start, and it might even give us an opportunity to license the technology down the road. We might just see noise-canceling television audio in a few years. Of course, that might disturb the news channels," he chuckled.

"I figure that we can afford to do only one of these, but I'll have to ask the shareholders about that." Will knew that Mike was the only shareholder that mattered, including some of the older guys in the shop. In fact, Mike and the other senior employees were the only shareholders. Mike continued, "I know that our primary concern is the risk of these alternatives. We don't want to get burned again, and we don't want to bite off more than we can chew. For each proposal, we've given you three or four different sales and cost scenarios, and I've been over them several times looking for holes. None of these ideas would be too taxing on our resources, and I don't think they would cannibalize existing sales. They're just so unrelated to each other and to what we're already doing that I don't see a way of sorting out which one would have the best chance of success. Maybe your Magic Spreadsheet can tell us which way to go."

In fact, Will had already summarized the numbers for the three projects, but he wanted to get a better understanding of the reliability of the scenario information before giving Mike his recommendation (Exhibit 1). In addition, he had decided to judge Mike's enthusiasm for each proposal one more time, at this meeting.

Exhibit 1. Sound Products, Inc. 2002 Capital Budget Development.
Results of Scenario Analysis

Project Title	Best Case	Most Likely Case	Almost-Worst Case	Worst Case
Turntable project:				
Net Present Value	$500,000.00	$210,000.00		-$90,000.00
scenario probability	0.25	0.40		0.35
Car Audio project:				
Net Present Value	$315,000.00	$175,000.00	-$75,000.00	-$100,000.00
scenario probability	0.30	0.35	0.25	0.10
Noise project:				
Net Present Value		$435,000.00	-$121,000.00	-$135,000.00
scenario probability		0.55	0.35	0.10

From the look on Mike's face, that wasn't the end of new business. Given Mike's penchant for exposition, Will knew that there had to be more.

"And another thing: some of the unit heads and I were wondering how this decision was different from the type of investment decision that some big conglomerate would make, or the decision that you or I would make when deciding which stocks to pick for our portfolios. I know they're related, somehow, but we couldn't come up with the particulars."

Will knew there was still more.

Mike looked down and thought for a moment, taking a much-needed breath, and continued. "You know, Will, many of us have a great deal of time and effort invested in this company. I'm grateful for the work you're doing, and I hope we can work out some shares of stock for you pretty soon, too. But it's different for some of the guys on the shop floor; they've been here a while and they've got lots of equity, with dividends, plus they're drawing some hefty salaries to boot. Smitty, for one, was asking me just the other day about whether or not he has a good balance of investments with all that he's got tied up in this business. I told him to talk to you about it and you could set him straight on what's at stake. I know that's not quite part of your job description, but it would be nice to hear the opinion of a budding financial genius on something like that. If we need to take more out of this business and invest it elsewhere, for our own financial health, I expect you to be straight with me about it."

As often as Mike had surprised Will over the past few months, the last statement had been completely unexpected. Will sat up in his chair and looked across the desk. "Mike, I'll have something on this by the close of business Friday. For the last couple of issues, we might need to schedule some time for everyone to get together and discuss risk analysis and personal portfolio management."

"With you leading the discussion," the engineer quipped.

"Right. I'll try to set you folks straight on a few things." Will felt sure that his finance degree would serve him well in the next couple of days. As Mike stood to leave, he remarked to Will that it was good to have someone around who stayed on top of that kind of thing, for a change.

WILL STEVENS, FAMILY FINANCIAL CONSULTANT

At Sunday dinner, Will's parents had been ready to ask questions. In particular, his mother had asked about how she should allocate her 401k monies. In addition, her company had recently begun offering to sell stock to senior employees at a small discount from market value. She wondered whether or not she should be participating in this plan, and how much of her portfolio should be tied up in the shares, if any. She seemed hesitant to invest more of her wealth in the future of her firm, given the level of dedication and effort that she had put forth so far.

Will's dad was simply concerned about making sure he had the right balance of investments in his portfolio. He was worried that he was being too conservative, with retirement only a few years away.

Both parents looked to Will for answers, asking, "what would you do?" They knew he was only a beginner, but their confidence was endearing nonetheless. He planned to have a healthy discussion after dinner next Sunday to let them know what answers he had come up with.

WILL STEVENS, INDIVIDUAL INVESTOR

With all of the other questions to consider, Will had to decide about his own preferences for risk and his investment horizon. How should he allocate his portfolio? He knew that his age and income level entered into the solution, as well as the solutions to some of the other questions that had been posed to him. To start with, he had chosen a somewhat arbitrary mix for his own 401k plan at Sound Products, but he could modify this allocation once he had a better idea of what he *should* do. Maybe the answer was common sense, but with the hectic pace at work he was having trouble focusing on the "Big Picture." Answering this question might give him some insight into how the other folks in his life should think about things. He realized, too, that he'd be facing their situations soon enough.

He got up from his desk and stretched, grabbing his financial calculator, the production proposals and his analysis of each, and a fresh legal pad. His lucky pen had a fresh cartridge, and the conference room table was waiting. Perhaps he would clear up some items on that "To Do" list after all.

REQUIRED

1. After reviewing the results of his analysis, in Exhibit 1, Will had enough information to analyze the risk of each project. He knew that he should concentrate on measuring and comparing the "stand-alone" risk of each proposal. Develop an analysis of the stand-alone risk of the three proposals mentioned in the case. If the shareholders of Sound Products are primarily concerned about choosing the project with the least amount of risk, which project should be implemented?

2. Regarding Mike's question about the different contexts of risk, how is risk analysis for investment opportunities at a small firm (such as the mutually exclusive projects in the case) different from the type of risk analysis likely to be used by large, multinational firms? In particular, how does the availability of external capital such as publicly traded stock influence these decisions?

3. Given your answers to the prior questions, how and why should the process of risk analysis be different for an investor who was simply trying to determine which stocks to add to a well-diversified portfolio? How do the Capital Asset Pricing Model (CAPM) and other theories of investor behavior factor into the decision?

4. Mike seemed rather concerned about the question of whether or not the shareholders (and employees) of Sound Products had an appropriate balance in their investment portfolios, considering their large investment in the company. Discuss the costs and benefits of the shareholders' current positions, assuming that most of them are not well diversified. What

considerations should the employees make when voting to change the way the firm's income is distributed? What points should they think about when deciding how to allocate their own portfolios (between different types of outside investments and equity at Sound Products, for example)?

5. Will's mom and the folks in the shop seem to have asked different versions of the same question. His mom is faced with the opportunity to buy shares of the firm she works for, and she's worried that she may already have too large a part of her personal wealth invested in the company. Give several reasons why the company might be making this stock plan available to senior employees. Looking at your answer to Question 4, what tradeoffs must Will's mom recognize before choosing to invest in the stock of the company that she works for?

6. Will's mom and dad had asked, "what would you do?" Explain how an individual's age and income level should influence decisions about how much to invest and decisions about risk allocation among different types of investments. In particular, discuss how the investment objectives of various types of mutual funds (such as growth, growth and income, balanced growth, bond funds, etc.) might be more or less appropriate for individuals at different stages of their lives.

Case 23

RISKY BUSINESS

INTRODUCTION

Chuck Goetz III, part owner and CEO (chief executive officer) of Chuck Goetz Furniture, Inc. was fretting over the financial information of the firm. Goetz had assumed the CEO position in the prior year, even though his only management training was in human resources. He had been overwhelmed by the tremendous learning curve involved with the CEO position. His father, Charles Goetz, Jr., had died and left all of the shares in the firm to his heirs, only two of whom actually worked in the family business. Chuck knew that the family was supportive of his efforts (and struggles) with the CEO position, but also expected him to continue to provide them with hefty dividend checks. Chuck also wanted to do a good job simply because that was his work philosophy.

Chuck Goetz Furniture has manufactured wood and metal furniture for over 40 years. The firm sells furniture to retailers. Retail furniture houses usually have at least a 100% markup, necessary to provide them with a marketing/showroom/warehouse facility, and to provide profit above and beyond costs. Many retailers have a larger markup to offer "discounts" off of suggested retail, since "big sales" (discounts from suggested retail pricing) seems to attract people in for perceived bargains. The furniture retail business is fairly risky, and tends to rise and fall with economic conditions.

CHUCK'S DILEMMA

Chuck had been considering opening a retail outlet for Chuck Goetz Furniture, since the large markups were so attractive. He figured a sign with the company name would be memorable to potential customers, who would know that "Chuck *Gets* Furniture" for them! His accountant had developed an analysis of the expected cashflows and internal rate of return on the proposal, and had summarized these for Chuck. Although Chuck had dealt with investments in equipment and facilities, he had never considered investing in a business unit so different from the manufacturing business.

Chuck called an old friend of his, Frank Keene. Frank was a financial consultant with a prominent investment bank. Chuck figured Frank could at least suggest some methods for analyzing the proposed expansion. Frank was a long way from Conway, Arkansas, so Chuck didn't expect him to do the analysis for him. Chuck decided to give Frank a call.

Chuck entered Frank's cell phone number. "Frank Keene..." Frank answered.

"Frank, you rascal, how ya doin'? This is Chuck Goetz."

"Chuck who?," Frank kidded. "Just joking, Chuck. How are you? How is Arkansas these days?"

"Oh, OK. Things don't change much here, you know. Still going barefoot to the office!"

"Still can't afford shoes, eh? Whats up, man?"

"I was wondering if you could tell me how to analyze a project that isn't like our current business. We are a manufacturing company, but we're considering investing in a retail outlet. I know the basics of capital budgeting, but I don't know how to adjust the methods for a project with a different risk level." Chuck paused. Frank had taken a moment to yell at a summer intern.

"OK, go ahead. Just stamping out ignorance," Frank said.

"Well, if you can tell me what to research, I will. I know you're too involved to directly help me."

"Chuck, just look in some of your dad's finance textbooks. He always kept them on the lower shelf in his office. Look up 'risk adjusted discount rate,' or RADR, and 'certainty equivalent cash flow,' or CECF. What's your cost of funding the project?"

"The bank usually wants 8.25% APR, but more for this project, probably. I don't really know for equity, but it's probably around 15%, for our other projects, at least," Chuck said. "We use 48 percent debt and 52 percent equity."

"OK. Let's see...furniture retail...manufacturing..."Frank was rapidly typing on his computer. "Use a 4.5% premium for the RADR and a.." Frank paused, listening to a yell from across the room. "Let me email you. Gotta go." With that, Frank was off the line.

Chuck, after counting his blessings that he didn't have to work on Wall Street, awaited Frank's email. It came about an hour later (Exhibit 2). Chuck retrieved the cashflow and return analysis from the file (Exhibit 1) and sat down to try to figure out the adjustments.

Exhibit 1. Project Cashflow and Return.

Year	Net Cashflow	PVIF	PV
1	$2,569,000	0.865469365	$2,223,391
2	$3,220,000	0.749037221	$2,411,900
3	$3,220,000	0.648268768	$2,087,425
4	$3,220,000	0.561056759	$1,806,603
5	$3,220,000	0.485577437	$1,563,559
6	$3,220,000	0.420252396	$1,353,213
7	$3,220,000	0.363715574	$1,171,164
8	$3,220,000	0.314784687	$1,013,607
9	$3,220,000	0.272436503	$877,246
10	$3,220,000	0.235785447	$759,229
11	$3,220,000	0.204065081	$657,090
12	$3,220,000	0.176612076	$568,691
13	$3,220,000	0.152852341	$492,185
14	$3,220,000	0.132289019	$425,971
15	$3,220,000	0.114492093	$368,665
16	$3,220,000	0.099089399	$319,068
17	$3,220,000	0.085758839	$276,143
18	$3,220,000	0.074221648	$238,994
19	$3,220,000	0.064236563	$206,842
20	$3,220,000	0.055594777	$179,015
			$18,999,999

PROJECT COST: $19,000,000
INTERNAL RATE OF RETURN: 15.54424%

Exhibit 2. Email from Frank.

        Subject: Risk Adjustments
          From: "Frank Keene" <frank.keene4@pib.us.com>
          Date: Thu, February 19, 2004 10:08 am
      Priority: Normal
      Options: <u>View Full Header</u> | <u>View Printable Version</u> | <u>Add to Addressbook</u> | <u>View as HTML</u>

Chuck:

Use a 4 .5 % higher discount rate for the RADF method.

For the CECF approach, use the following:

year1: 96%	year11: 39%
year2: 91%	year12: 33%
year3: 85%	year13: 29%
year4: 79%	year14: 26%
year5: 74%	year15: 23%
year6: 68%	year16: 20%
year7: 62%	year17: 18%
year8: 56%	year18: 1 5%
year9: 50%	year19: 13%
year10: 45%	year20: 12%

Good Luck!

Frank

REQUIRED

1. Using the risk adjusted discount rate, assess the attractiveness of the project.

2. Using the certainty equivalent cashflow approach, assess the attractiveness of the project.

3. Do either of the adjustments change the decision? What would you recommend to Chuck?

SECTION 9

ENTREPRENEURIAL FINANCE

Case 24

CUSTOM LUMBER, INC.

INTRODUCTION

Custom Lumber, Inc. is a small, entrepreneurial venture that began in the summer of 1999 as a part time business. Its owner, Dave Stamin, is a warehouse manager for a furniture manufacturer in Spartanburg, South Carolina. Dave first began to produce lumber on a small scale one year prior to officially starting the business. In the beginning, it was just a hobby. Dave had heard of a brand of sawmill called a Wood Mizer, designed to be portable and efficient in terms of waste products. As a birthday treat when he turned 30, Dave purchased a sawmill for $11,898, and some accessory equipment for another $2,390 with some savings he had accumulated over several years. He had purchased the mill partly because he enjoyed the idea of producing something useful out of renewable resources, and partly because he wanted to gradually work out of the warehouse business into lumber production as a full time venture. His salary as a warehouse manager was not very good, he thought, at $42,000 per year, especially since he had a college degree in engineering. At the same time, he did not care to take a desk job in engineering, and he sure loved the outdoors. He thought that the sawmill could be a solution. At this point in his life, he had no family to support and no debt to speak of. It seemed like an ideal time to start the venture full time.

THE PART TIME BUSINESS

At first, Dave had only cut lumber from his own trees. Dave owned a small tract of land outside of Spartanburg, worth approximately $150,000. He had done a surprisingly large volume of production just for his own use, like fencing, log barns, and rough framing timbers. In June of 1999, however, he decided that he wanted to make a business out of it, so he applied for a business license and began custom cutting jobs for other people, charging by the hour for his labor and for use of the specialized equipment. The Wood Mizer used a cantilevered bandsaw that cut the length of the log, with little waste because of the thin bandsaw blade. He pulled the mill behind his pickup truck, and found that the portability actually increased his business. Wherever he cut for a customer, the milling drew a big crowd and additional jobs.

167

FINANCIAL INFORMATION

Dave charged a setup fee of $50 per job, and a standard hourly rate of $20 to compensate himself, plus the cost of saw blades, gasoline, and other materials used. If Dave encountered nails or other foreign objects in the sawlogs that ruined his blade, the customer paid for a new blade ($19 each). Dave's customers were very satisfied with this arrangement, because they could have custom timber cut from their sawlogs at about a fourth the price of purchasing the lumber at the lumberyard.

Dave's monthly financial records appear in Exhibit 1. The results are based completely on cash basis, although Dave was able to reduce his tax burden by depreciating his sawmill and accessory equipment. His accountant had recommended using the Modified Accelerated Cost Recovery System (MACRS) depreciation method. Dave's 1999 depreciation expense is summarized in Exhibit 2.

In February 2000, Dave began wondering if the sawmill business was sufficient to support him financially if he did it full time. Dave lived by himself and had no family to support. The land he now owned had been left to him by his parents, both of whom had died three years ago. He already had a lot of the equipment he would need for the business. However, a loan from the bank would be necessary to expand the business. He figured the business would be organized as a subchapter S corporation. He needed the loan to provide for new equipment (Exhibit 3) and for cash ($3,000) and supplies ($2,000).

Dave constructed a worksheet summarizing his equipment and its 'book' value based on the depreciation he had accumulated so far. This worksheet appears in Exhibit 2. He also figured out the additional equipment he needed to 'make a go of it' (Exhibit 3) and the additional expenses he expected to incur from having a workshop and hiring two full time helpers (Exhibit 4). Dave's accountant agreed that the numbers seemed reasonable and accurate.

Dave had shopped around for loan rates, and decided that his current banker, Tom Landers, had given him the best quotes and seemed easy to work with. He nervously dialed Tom's number. Tom's secretary answered, and connected them. "Hello, Tom," Dave began. "I think I'm ready to go ahead with the loan we discussed."

"Well, it's about time. I think the idea is a great one. You need to bring some cost and income estimates with you - actually, there's a list of items," Tom replied. Dave waited as Landers rummaged through his files. "Ah, here it is. You will need to bring the information about the jobs you did as a part timer, so we can see how profitable it has been as a hobby business. You also need to bring in some profit and loss forecasts. Just list the revenues you expect to make and deduct all your costs. Be sure to include your depreciation expenses. You can hold off on interest on the debt, since that depends on whether or not you borrow the money."

"Will the loan be secured by the equipment," Dave asked?

"No, we'll just use your land as collateral, and that will get you a better interest rate, probably about nine percent. We'll set the loan up on an annual payment, so you won't have to start paying it back so soon" replied Landers. "How many days per month do you think you can cut?"

Dave thought for a moment. He would probably work six days a week, weather permitting. It rained about two days per week, normally, so he figured four days a week would be a conservative estimate. "Maybe twenty days a month," he replied.

IMMEDIATE FUTURE OF THE BUSINESS

Dave had at least twenty jobs lined up for the business, with an average of 3-4 days of work (at 8 hours per day) for each job, assuming he hired two assistants. He would likely be at least three times as productive if he hired the two assistants. The handling tasks, which they would be doing, were the most time consuming activity. The three of them could keep the mill cutting lumber all the time, whereas before, he had to stop to do the handling tasks. These involved custom cutting work like he had been doing, at the same prices he had quoted before.

He also perceived that, in case of financial need, he could cut his own black oak trees and sell the green lumber to a local lumberyard that had a lumber kiln drier. If he did this, he estimated that most of the proceeds would be profit, since he didn't have to pay for the sawlogs, and the gasoline and blade wear were relatively insignificant. Dave had about 240 large black oak trees he could cut and saw if he had to. The green lumber would bring about $300 per tree, after expenses, at the local kiln. He would only do this in the unlikely event he did not get any more custom cutting jobs after the initial ones.

Dave was certain that he could continue to acquire business that would keep him busy continually, though. There appeared to be plenty of demand for the work. The first step, though, was to gather the information required by the bank for the loan.

THE FORECAST

Dave decided to take a day off from work to assemble the required estimates. He got out some ledger paper that Landers had given him. "Let's see," he thought to himself. "Profit and Loss statements, and how I can repay the loan..." Dave paused for a moment, thinking about the business as a full time venture. He thought about the loan from the bank's perspective. If he were in Landers' position, would he approve the loan? Why or why not? Did he really have to pledge his acreage as collateral? Why did Landers not even consider using the equipment as collateral? Was this venture really good for him, and would it justify quitting his job, which at least had a steady paycheck? Was he taking an inadvisable amount of risk by doing the project?

Dave's head began spinning. It seemed that there would be a substantial amount of detail involved with the estimates. He decided to start with constructing a balance sheet of the assets he had now, plus what he proposed to buy. The only debt would be what he borrowed from the bank for the additional assets. The forecast of an income statement was also in order. Landers also wanted cashflow figures, which had to take into account depreciation and its effect on taxes. Landers had given him a cashflow worksheet to fill out (Exhibit 5) after he had done the forecasted income statement.

Exhibit 1. Monthly Financial Records.

	Fee Income	Expenses	Profit
June 1999 (21 hours)	$640	$124	$516
July 1999 (20 hours)	$680	$102	$578
August 1999 (15 hours)	$540	$108	$432
September 1999 (39 hours)	$1,080	$209	$871
October 1999 (36 hours)	$945	$187	$758
November 1999 (32 hours)	$920	$170	$750
December 1999 (12 hours)	$520	$92	$428
January 2000 (44 hours)	$1,250	$421	$829
February 2000 (36 hours)	$1,220	$262	$958
TOTAL	$7,795	$1,675	$6,120

Exhibit 2. Book Values of Assets.

	Cost	1999 Deprec.	Book Value
LT-40G24 Portable Sawmill	$13,890.00	$1,984.88	$11,905.12
Blade Maintenance Pkg (sharpener)	$1,908.00	$272.65	$1,635.35
Cant Hooks (2@43.50 ea)	$87.00	$29.00	$58.00
Chain Saws (2@328 ea)	$652.00	$217.31	$434.69
Log Carriage	$849.00	$121.32	$727.68
Honda 4WD ATV	$7,830.00	$1,118.91	$6,711.09
TOTALS	$25,216.00	$3,744.07	$21,471.93

Exhibit 3. Additional Equipment Needed.

Edging Machine (7-year MACRS)	$3,085
Sharpening Bench (5-year MACRS)	$458
Work Stools (2@54 ea) (5-year MACRS)	$108
Mill Upgrade (Hydraulic) (7-year MACRS)	$3,208
Lumber Storage Racks (7-year MACRS)	$8,865
TOTAL	$15,724

Exhibit 4. Expected Increases in Expenses.

Monthly Expense Categories	Amount
Labor (2 workers*20days*8hrs*$10/hr)	$3,200
Insurance	$183
Utilities	$200
Gasoline	$250
Mill expenses	$220
TOTAL	$4,053

Exhibit 5: Annual Cashflow Worksheet.

EBIT   _____

X (1-MTR*)   _____

+ DEPRECIATION EXPENSE   _____

= NET OPERATING CASHFLOW   _____

*(Marginal tax rate (MTR) is tax expense as a percentage of EBIT)

REQUIRED

1. Develop a beginning balance sheet for the company using information in the case and in Exhibits 1 and 2. Assume that the loan is used for financing the new equipment.

2. Develop a proforma income statement for the first month of operation using the production, fee income, cost, and expense information in the case.

3. Is the operating cashflow adequate to repay the loan? Is it adequate to provide a living for Dave? How would you advise Dave in terms of both the decision and concerning financing?

SECTION 10

BANKING CREDIT DECISIONS

Case 25

JONESVILLE CANDY COMPANY

The last few years had been quite exciting for the folks at the Jonesville Candy Company. They had been successful in starting and "growing" a small business, which put them ahead of most small business owners. In addition, Jonesville Candy had received national recognition several years ago from an article in a regional decorating magazine and this publicity had helped them to expand sales and the company's markets each year.

Jonesville Candy Company (JCC) was located in the Ozark mountains of western Arkansas. It had been started as a small, part-time family business many years before, but the family had decided that the firm should be incorporated at the end of the 2000 season. The company produced many different varieties of hard candies, stick candies, nuts and fudge, and it sold these products at retail locations, via a catalog and online. It had recently been very successful with its wholesale private label products. These products allowed large customers to choose a certain group of candies or nuts and have thousands of units made-to-order with special packaging. These packages would then be sent out as a gift from the customer or as a premium for buying one of the customer's products. The folks at JCC were hopeful that this type of exclusive product would become even more popular as time went by. In addition, the private label products were very good at promoting JCC to new customers.

THE ADVANTAGES OF YOUTH

Earl Jones was the grandchild of the company's founders, and he had spent his youth helping to make and sell candy in the Jonesville area. Back then, sales had been done on an honor basis; if you took the product, there was a jar for your payment on the counter. Earl had fond memories of those days, mainly because back then someone else had made the decisions for the company.

At age 28, Earl was the chief financial officer of Jonesville Candy. After graduating from business school in Little Rock, he'd spent a few years in the "real world" working as a commercial loan officer at a regional bank. The company also employed an accounting staff, of course, but the family wanted to have someone to look out for their interests and to make sure that the company was growing in the right ways. Earl understood this; the accountants were busy just keeping up with how much sugar the company had used last month. The future, to them, was anything past the end of this week. Earl relied on the accountants for help, and they had been more than willing to have someone with the family's confidence come on board.

Recently, Earl had become convinced that private label products and catalog sales of high margin specialties were the most attractive growth opportunities for the company, and he had convinced the board of directors (two uncles, three aunts, and his parents) that JCC should work to expand its business and capacity for these products. To this end, he planned to have JCC sales representatives begin attending more business-to-business conferences, wholesale product conventions and holiday product showcases. He planned to hire several advertising firms to develop specialized campaigns for JCC which would promote these products and help JCC understand the customers it was trying to sell to. In discussing his plan with his advertising consultants, Earl had discovered that the majority of the additional marketing expense would come within the first year (2005). Earl planned to ask a local bank for a small loan in order to offset some of this anticipated marketing expense and to help establish the company's credit rating.

A FINANCIAL CRYSTAL BALL

From his years as a loan officer, Earl realized that one of the most important factors in obtaining a loan was the firm's forecast of future operations. Loan officers were trained to look for profitability, of course, but they wanted to know how any loan would be used and also whether it could be repaid from operating cash flows over time. Earl had already compiled several years of balance sheet figures (Exhibit 1), along with JCC's income and cash flow statement information (Exhibits 2 and 3).

Exhibit 1. Balance Sheets for years ending December 31.

	12/31/2002	12/31/2003	12/31/2004
Cash	$162,474	$238,429	$316,525
Accounts Receivable	$205,506	$211,671	$218,021
Inventory	$210,027	$216,328	$222,818
Gross Fixed Assets	$525,000	$525,000	$525,000
less: Accumulated Depreciation	$26,923	$40,385	$53,846
Net Fixed Assets	$498,077	$484,615	$471,154
Total Assets	$1,076,084	$1,151,044	$1,228,518
Accounts Payable	$75,240	$77,497	$79,822
Equity (100,000 shares)	$1,000,844	$1,073,546	$1,148,696
Total Liab. & Equity, Preliminary	$1,076,084	$1,151,043	$1,228,518
Loan Needs (Marketable Securities)	$0	$0	$0
Total Liab. & Equity, Adjusted	$1,076,084	$1,151,044	$1,228,518
Change in Loan Needs	$0	$0	$0

Exhibit 2. Income Statements for years ending December 31.

	12/31/2002	12/31/2003	12/31/2004
Sales	$1,500,195	$1,545,201	$1,591,557
Cost of Goods Sold	$1,050,137	$1,081,641	$1,114,090
Gross Margin	$450,059	$463,560	$477,467
Operating Expenses	$330,043	$339,944	$350,143
Depreciation Expense	$13,462	$13,462	$13,462
Special Marketing Expense	$0	$0	$0
Total Operating Expenses	$343,504	$353,406	$363,604
Earnings Before Taxes	$106,554	$110,155	$113,863
less: Taxes @ 34%	$36,228	$37,453	$38,713
Earnings After Taxes	$70,326	$72,702	$75,150
Taxable Income	$106,554	$110,155	$113,863
Tax Loss Carry	$0	$0	$0
Dividends paid	$0	$0	$0

Exhibit 3. Cash-based Income Statements for years ending December 31.

	12/31/2002	12/31/2003	12/31/2004
Cash Sales:			
Net Sales	$1,500,195	$1,545,201	$1,591,557
less: Change in A/R	($5,986)	($6,165)	($6,350)
Total Cash Receipts	$1,494,209	$1,539,036	$1,585,207
Cash Disbursements:			
COGS	($1,050,137)	($1,081,641)	($1,114,090)
less: Change in Inventory	($6,117)	($6,301)	($6,490)
plus: Change in A/P	$4,117	$2,257	$2,325
Total Cash Purchases	($1,052,137)	($1,085,684)	($1,118,255)
Total Operating Expenses	($343,504)	($353,406)	($363,604)
plus: Depreciation Expense	$13,462	$13,462	$13,462
less: Taxes Paid	($36,228)	($37,453)	($38,713)
Total Cash Disbursements	($1,418,408)	($1,463,081)	($1,507,111)
Cash Flow From (Used By) Operations	$75,801	$75,955	$78,096
Capital Expenditures	$0	$0	$0
New Stock and/or LTD	$0	$0	$0
Dividends Paid			
Change in Loan Needs	$0	$0	$0
Derived Change in Cash	$75,801	$75,955	$78,096
Actual Change in Cash	$75,801	$75,955	$78,096

Predicting the future was a difficult task, but Earl had good estimates of how things would change in the forecasted years. In the past, the accounts receivable balance had represented approximately fifty days of average daily revenues, and because of pressure from customers and the new type of customers being recruited it was thought that this amount would grow to sixty days' worth of daily sales. Inventory turnover, which was more closely related to the company's cost of goods sold than revenues, would increase from 3.5 times per year to 5 times. After widely-varying cash balances in the past, Earl determined that JCC only needed to maintain a cash balance of $112,500 each year, and he would include this in the forecast.

He also anticipated that accounts payable days outstanding would decrease from 26 in the past to 25 days going forward. Earl planned to forecast this account by multiplying average daily purchases (the sum of the cost of goods sold number and the change in inventory, divided by 365 days) by the new A/P days outstanding number. To him, this method appeared to be more accurate than using a simple percentage of COGS or sales.

On the income statement, Earl and his family were confident that sales could continue to grow approximately three percent each year. As discussed, the mix of sales was changing, and this change would have its own set of effects, although the firm's gross margin was expected to remain the same as well. Operating expenses would probably increase to approximately 25 percent of revenues beginning in 2005, but the company's fixed assets were being depreciated over a long period of time so he didn't expect that expense to change during the forecasted years. Even with the recent move to reduce marginal tax rates at the federal level, Earl anticipated that JCC would continue to pay taxes at a 34 percent average rate. Any projected losses, though, would be carried forward to reduce the company's income tax liability in the future.

The company's new marketing efforts would cost $92,500 in the first year and approximately $12,100 in each of the years following. For presentation purposes and to stress its importance, Earl had decided to give this expense its own line on his forecasted income statements.

Finally, Earl had promised the family that the business would begin to pay dividends in fiscal 2005. It had never paid dividends in the past, but it was decided to start with a special dividend of $0.75 per share in the first year and then to pay $0.25 per share in the following years.

Again, Earl knew that the loan decision depended upon the timing and size of cash flows from the ordinary course of business. He designed his cash flow statement very carefully to make sure that a banker would be able to see "Cash Flow From (Used By) Operations." Although it was rare that bankers would depend upon the liquidation of collateral in a loan analysis, he also planned to forecast a collateral schedule similar to what he had developed in the past (Exhibit 4).

Exhibit 4. Jonesville Candy Company; Historical Collateral Schedule.

	12/31/2002	12/31/2003	12/31/2004
Cash	$162,474	$238,429	$316,525
Accounts Receivable (at 60%)	$123,304	$127,003	$130,813
Inventory (at 70%)	$147,019	$151,430	$155,973
Building, Improvements (at 70% of historical co	$367,500	$367,500	$367,500
Total Collateral Amount Available	$800,297	$884,361	$970,810
Loan from the bank	$0	$0	$0
Loan-to-Value Ratio	N/A	N/A	N/A
Collateral Coverage Ratio	N/A	N/A	N/A

Earl was certain that the company faced a bright future, and all of the recent attention had made everyone in the company feel better about things and work a little harder. As he sat down at his computer to finish his forecasts, he grabbed a few of JCC's "All Natural Old Timey Brand" cough drops to munch on. A sugar rush was always good for helping him think.

REQUIRED

1. Develop a forecast of Jonesville's balance sheets and income statements starting with the next fiscal year (2005) and ending with 2009. In order to make your total assets equal total liabilities and equity, you may need to create a line item entitled "Loan Needs," as shown in the case exhibits. In periods that the firm is expected to have an excess of liabilities and equity over total assets, label this excess "Marketable Securities." (Note: because the case should focus on the loan timing and the amount needed, you should ignore any interest expense associated with a new loan at this stage of your analysis.)

2. Using the balance sheets and income statements generated in response to 1, above, develop projected cash flow statements similar to those in Exhibit 3. (In your forecast, the "derived change in cash" should equal the "actual change in cash" across each period from the projected balance sheet.)

3. According to the projections developed for the prior questions, how much money will JCC need to borrow from its bank, and when will it need these funds

4. According to the projections from Questions 1 and 2, when will JCC be able to begin repaying any loan that it may need to obtain?

5. In the case, Earl suggests that the most desirable source of funds for repaying a loan would be "cash flow from operations." Given your analyses for the prior questions, will JCC generate enough cash in the normal course of business to repay any bank loans that it needs? What other sources of repayment might be available?

6. The case mentions that banks won't usually rely upon the liquidation of collateral for the eventual repayment of a loan. What characteristics determine whether or not a bank will accept a particular asset as collateral? Why does Earl's collateral schedule (Exhibit 4) use only part of the value of each asset category (such as sixty percent of accounts receivable)? What is meant by the "Loan-to-Value" and "Collateral Coverage" ratios in the exhibit, and would these be useful to bankers?

7. What are the "5 Cs of credit?" How are some of these characteristics reflected in financial statements? Which characteristics may not be reflected in financial statements at all? How would one go about evaluating those characteristics that aren't easily related in the financial documents of a firm?

8. Question 1 asks you to ignore the effects of interest costs on the balance sheets and income statements you are projecting. Without making any additional calculations, explain the linkages between the income statement and the balance sheet and how interest costs would change your projections.

SECTION 11

DIVIDEND POLICY

Case 26

HAVELOCHE CORPORATION

INTRODUCTION

Phil Grange, the CEO of Haveloche Corporation, has been asked to be a guest lecturer at Cokesbury College. One of the finance professors has specifically requested a discussion on Haveloche's dividend policy. In preparation, Phil has reviewed several textbooks that Dr. Roche, the professor, has provided, and has printed out the history of dividends for the nine years that Haveloche Corporation has been publicly traded.

BACKGROUND

Haveloche Corporation was formed in 1989 as a research firm dedicated to innovative electronic design. Haveloche sells patents to large electronics manufacturing companies. For innovative inventions that are immediately useful to these electronics firms, Haveloche receives handsome gains. Many of the inventions and patents also wind up sitting on a shelf, even after Haveloche goes to the effort and expense of gaining the patent. Inventions that hit the jackpot make up for the losers over time, but the successes are sporadic and create large fluctuations in Haveloche's earnings.

The firm grew very quickly until its initial public offering in June of 1994 due to several key patents that were snatched up by several large computer manufacturers. By 1994, there were 28 researchers in the Haveloche think-tank, and the firm had developed the reputation for cutting edge research with a market orientation. Haveloche was also one of the larger pure research firms, and appeared to have become large enough to ensure more frequent innovations and earnings that were not as volatile as smaller firms. Since the IPO, Haveloche's research capability grew until a high of 102 researchers was reached. In early 2001, Haveloche had to reduce workloads and eventually had to reduce the number of researchers due to the economic downturn. Since early 2003, though, the firm seemed to be enjoying the high demand again, and expanded in order to take advantage of the upsurge.

PAST DIVIDEND PRACTICES

Haveloche's fiscal year ends in June each year, at which point the firm pays dividends, if any. From the initial public offering of stock until 2000, Haveloche pursued a dividend policy of paying out 20% of earnings in cash dividends. In January 2000, Phil Grange took over the CEO position at Haveloche and began to vary the dividend based on the firm's need for cash reinvestment. If the firm had need of equity funding, the cash dividends were lowered, which was usually the case. A few times, dividends were relatively high, since an immediate capital need was not present.

Phil had reviewed materials that Professor Roche had given him, and had refreshed his memory on several theories of dividend policy. The concepts seemed to be inconclusive at best, and the textbooks seemed to ramble through opinions from a variety of perspectives. The ideal dividend policy was not identified, though. Phil was unsure of how to even approach his talk, considering the textbooks couldn't even seem to draw a conclusion. He decided to just present Haveloche's history along with the stock price over time and answer any questions that arose during the class period.

Phil decided to just learn as much as he could about the different hypotheses concerning dividend policy, so that he could easily refer to them in his responses to questions. He sent an email to Professor Roche indicating his intentions for presentation, and got a response back that those ideas were fine. Phil listed dividends paid and the firm's stock price for every year of its public operation. Usually, the dividend was announced publicly about a month ahead of payment. Phil figured the daily prices before and after the announcement events might be interesting to discuss, as well, so he made a table of those values. Phil emailed the data to Professor Roche, with the suggestion that the students use the data to come up with some preliminary arguments concerning what policy they thought was supported or refuted. He figured he could spend an entire class period reviewing dividend policy in general, and then having students interpret their analysis of the numbers.

Exhibit 1. Dividend and Stock Price, years 1994-2003.

Year	Dividend	Price
94	$0.33	$44.12
95	$1.33	$60.50
96	$0.75	$64.25
97	$1.65	$41.12
98	$2.23	$65.10
99	$2.60	$59.00
00	$2.18	$74.50
01	$1.30	$66.25
02	$1.10	$81.12
03	$1.70	$75.50

Exhibit 2. Stock Price.
One Day Prior to and One Day After Dividend Announcements.

Year	Price (t-1)	Price (t+1)
94	$42.50	$43.00
95	$60.50	$60.25
96	$63.12	$63.75
97	$41.50	$40.87
98	$66.12	$64.90
99	$58.75	$59.12
00	$74.50	$74.37
01	$63.22	$63.24
02	$79.45	$81.24
03	$76.02	$75.98

REQUIRED

1. Enter the data from Exhibits 1 and 2 into a spreadsheet program. Graph a scatter plot of the dividend with the stock price. Does there appear to be a correlation?

2. Plot the change in price (from t-1 to t+1) with the dividend amount. Does there appear to be a correlation? Plot the change in price with the year to year change in the dividend. Does there appear to be a correlation?

3. Summarize the implications of each dividend hypothesis/theory found in your financial management textbooks. Which one explains what is going on with Haveloche?

4. When the dividend was increased, did the stock price tend to react favorably or unfavorably? Why might either result occur?

5. What would you suggest to Phil concerning what type of dividend policy to pursue? Justify your answer.